Break on Through

Break on Through

Surviving Autism

Constance Porter, RN

iUniverse, Inc.
New York   Bloomington

Break on Through
Surviving Autism

iUniverse books may be ordered through booksellers or by contacting:

iUniverse
1663 Liberty Drive
Bloomington, IN 47403
www.iuniverse.com
1-800-Authors (1-800-288-4677)

ISBN: 978-0-595-47902-3(pbk)
ISBN: 978-0-595-60051-9(ebk)
ISBN: 978-0-595-71397-4(cloth)

Printed in the United States of America
iUniverse rev. date: 4/20/09

This book is dedicated to all of those whose lives have been impacted by autism.

The proceeds from this book will be donated to the Autism Research Foundation.

Autism

Even before I was born,
From your world I was being torn.

When I was just a little guy,
Growth in my brain had gone awry.

With you was where I wanted to stay,
Blue suddenly, I began to slip away.

Now my world comes crashing in.
Too much. Too fast. I can't contend.
I block it out. I fend it off.
I can't. I scream. I run off.

The different things that bring me glee
Seem odd to those who stare at me.

I try to bring order to my concrete life
That's filled with much frustration and strife.

Though my behaviors don't concur
With the little boy who lives next door,
I need your help to open doors,
To let my life be more like yours.

Understanding is the key
To offer hope for those like me.

Constance Porter

1995

Contents

Acknowledgments

My tireless and infinitely patient editor, Laura, a high school honors English teacher, offered to be my editor when I told her the idea that became this book. I would never have had the gumption to begin this project without her help and support. She unmixed my metaphors, undangled my participles, and somehow made clear my often garbled ramblings. Her high expectations and gentle nudging kept me on task. I thank her immensely.

My wonderful husband, Rex, offered steadfast support throughout the entire process and, along with Michele and Jill and big bro Jan, suffered through the early drafts of the inchoate manuscript. I thank them all for their help and encouragement.

There are so many good people I have gotten to meet over the years because of Derek: Connie, Dan, Adam, Vic, Kat, Sandy, Katrina, Kelly, Kyle, Jill, John, Gary, Robin, Barb, Kim, Nancy, Maura, Karen, Wanda, Michelle, Candace, Patty, Jenny, Dee, and of course, our Michele.

And whether Derek knows it or not, there have been many remarkable classmates at every level that I consider his friends. They easily forgave Derek for whatever antics he put them through and always had a friendly smile for us: Andy and his mom, Sue; Erica; J.C.; Stephanie; Chris; Laura; Sarah; Brandon; Billy and his mom, Sandy; Donovan; Kyle; Ryan; and Chelsea. I love them all.

I also need to acknowledge those who helped our family when times were especially tough, namely the Yates, Slater, Mills, Romano and Will families, and the entire Gonzagza Prep community.

Introduction

By all outward appearances, we are a typical family. My husband, Rex, and I live with our three children in Spokane, Washington. Rex is an anesthesiologist, and I work as a teacher's aide and part-time nurse in our school district. Our daughter, Whitney, is a sophomore in college, and our sons, Derek and Dylan, are high school students. Three cats, a dog, and a bird make our family complete. The one point, however, that may set us apart from other "typical" families is that Derek has autism. This book is an account of Derek's experiences, as well as an account of our family's life with Derek.

I've based this book only on my son's experiences. It is an honest account of our daily lives with Derek. Attempting to write a book in the somewhat controlled chaos that is often my home has been quite a feat. I largely wrote it on fast-food napkins while sitting in the car with my autistic son, waiting for his brother at the many sports camps he attended this summer. While enjoying the quiet contemplation, I would jot down thoughts, memories, and ideas as they came to me. I did research and expanded my notes in the early morning hours until the compilation took form. I hope our experiences will resonate with other families who have similar challenges; perhaps this book will also give them some insight into raising a child with autism.

My hope when beginning this endeavor was to write a book that would be of use to those with newly diagnosed children—people who are desperate for relevant information, as I was after Derek was diagnosed with autism. At that time, I found one of my main sources of strength in the pages of *The Siege*, written in 1967 by Clara Claiborne Park. In it, Park recounts her own battle with her daughter's autism, in a time when precious little information about the condition was available. I so admire the perseverance and dedication that this gifted author demonstrated. She was a beacon for me and a parent whom I would aspire to become.

This book is not an account of why my child is special. Derek has not impacted the world any more or less than any other person with autism. We are just the Porter family—an imperfect but functional group of distinct individuals who have found their own ways to cope with Derek's autism. Derek's autism has become a part of all of us and has changed who we are. Reality emerges when pain is fully felt and absorbed into the fiber of our lives.

Autism is a lifelong neurologic disorder that is usually apparent in the first two years of the child's life. It is characterized by deficits in speech, cognition, language, social interactions, and sensory integration. Early intervention is important to achieve maximum impact for improvement.

The impetus of this book was inspired by William Faulkner's *The Sound and the Fury*, a book that resonated with me even before Derek was born. It is the story of beautiful Caddy Compson and her tragic dysfunctional family, as told from different perspectives by her three brothers—developmentally delayed Benjy, neurotic Quentin, and evil Jason. It is rather depressing and, in my opinion, should be read backwards. Nevertheless, I enjoyed the different takes on the same theme. I wanted to use this method in presenting some of our experiences with Derek to show how misunderstood those with autism and their families can be.

In high school, I was once required to memorize a passage from Shakespeare's *Macbeth*. It has stayed with me over the years and seems particularly poignant now. It is from this passage that Faulkner titled his nihilistic classic:

> Tomorrow, and tomorrow, and tomorrow
>
> Creeps in this petty pace from day to day
>
> To the last syllable of recorded time,
>
> And all our yesterdays have lighted fools
>
> The way to dusty death. Out, out, brief candle.
>
> Life's but a walking shadow, a poor player
>
> That struts and frets his hour upon the stage,
>
> And then is heard no more. It is a tale
>
> Told by an idiot, full of sound and fury,
>
> Signifying nothing.

So here we are, creeping in this petty pace, while Derek is full of trapped sound and fury. Day to day we are all just trying to signify something. The meaning of life is to try to make your life meaningful. I believe that has been Derek's gift to us.

Chapter 1

PERSPECTIVES AND PERCEPTIONS

A Marvelous Night for a Moon Dance

Darkness to me means freedom. No watchful eyes, no angry stares, no portions, no restraints, no demands. I love the calm quiet of the night. The blaring lights and noises fade. I'm gleeful in my temporary freedom from my other world. I disrobe in rebellion and dance in the coolness of the night. Garments glide gracefully down from the balcony. Chairs tumble and twirl, catching the moonlight before bouncing, then resting awkwardly. The plants sail straight down, landing with a satisfying, audible thud. The railing has a pleasant resonance that reverberates when I tap on it with my shoe.

But my sister brought me in after the angry men came, and mom gave me some bitter juice to drink. Soon I felt sleepy and was carried to bed to sleep with Dad.

When we were in Mexico, we stayed next to this really strange family. They were a trip. This crazy kid was dancing around naked on the third-floor balcony in the middle of the night. He was throwing all kinds of shit into the courtyard. It's lucky he didn't kill someone. After about five calls down to the desk, the cops finally came. Hopefully, they hauled the little weirdo off.

----

re^ zz

I was awakened by loud, deliberate knocking. I squinted at the clock, which read 2:23. I opened the door to find two angry men in uniform holding patio furniture and pajamas and underwear that strangely resembled Derek's. I yelled for Whitney, who had been sleeping in the same room as her brothers, to check on Derek. The officers spoke in loud, rapid Spanish that I couldn't understand. I hadn't used any of my limited Spanish since leaving Miami about thirty years ago. Fear quickly cleared the fog of sleep from my brain, and my mind raced as I struggled to say "autism" in Spanish. From somewhere in the cobwebbed recesses of my brain, a phrase in Spanish surfaced that I didn't even know I knew: "Mi hijo es idiota."

That seemed to be all the explanation the men needed. As Derek emerged from the back bedroom sans clothes, they stopped yelling, put the clothing and furniture down in front of the doorway, and left. I was happy and relieved that our trip did not include a stay in a Mexican jail. This vacation with Derek was anything but.

This was during the summer of 2000, when Rex and I decided to take the family on a trip to Puerto Vallarta. When the kids were younger and our lives were simpler, we took a family trip every year, usually to Florida because of the family and friends there. A new destination seemed like a good idea as we sat around the dining room table leafing through glossy travel brochures that featured gorgeous, expansive white beaches with tall palm trees and radiant sunsets. A tropical vacation would provide a nice break from our dreary Northwest winter weather. I could almost smell the ocean and taste the fresh seafood.

With the exception of a twelve-hour meltdown at Disney World when Derek was about five, he had always been a well-behaved traveler. Although we always have concerns about exposing Derek to people he has never met or people who do not know about autism, these had always been minor issues, up until this trip. Derek had periodic outbursts that could startle those who didn't know of his condition; but for the most part, he was well behaved on prior excursions and we had no reason to believe this trip would be any different. Our thoughts were confirmed on the uneventful plane ride to Puerto Vallarta, where Derek was sweet and compliant. The customs officials easily accepted our travel documents, and any remaining stress melted away as our parched, pasty white bodies sucked up the warm, muggy air like sponges. We followed the color-coded lines painted on the airport floor to a line of waiting taxis. For mere pesos, we were whisked off to our hotel. Our vacation had officially begun.

We settled into our room and began to plan our itinerary, eagerly plowing through the hotel literature and planning each jam-packed day—careful not to miss a single excursion. The dolphin adventure was a must. So was the pirate cruise, snorkeling on the reef, a scenic horseback ride in the Sierra Madres, a bus excursion to Panta Mita beach, and a tequila distillery tour. We prioritized all the recommended restaurants and decided on one for our first night's dinner. After the long day of travel, we were all so famished that we broke all our agreed-upon rules at our first meal: we drank the water and ate the fruit and the vegetables. After all, we're made of strong stock; *tourista* is for sissies.

Derek was the first to get it. He wasn't outwardly ill at first— just a little warm and more subdued than usual. Rex and I could tell that he wasn't himself on one of the first days of our Mexican adventure, but he was still docile and curious. Our first stop was the dolphin adventure, where visitors get pulled around a large pool by tame bottlenose dolphins. We took a short cab ride to an area where we were to be loaded onto safari shuttles. While waiting

3

to board, Derek bolted toward a shade tree to lie down on a bed of gravel. My instincts said to sit there with him and send his brother, sister, and Rex along without us. I have very good instincts and know it is always a mistake to ignore them. But Whitney, thirteen, and Dylan, eight, were going to *swim with dolphins*; how could I not watch that?

I picked up Derek, and onto the safari bus we went. Thankfully, it was a short ride. Our small group disembarked and waited for further instruction at the entrance gate. Not even a minute elapsed when Derek covered a fellow adventurer with projectile vomit. She was as gracious as one could be under the circumstances, and thankfully there were showers nearby. The water rinsed off some, but the vomit stuck tenaciously, as did the acrid cloud surrounding us. The awful smell lingered throughout the excursion. I carried Derek to a shaded bench, where he lay prostrate and motionless until his siblings finished their "adventure." Every attempt to hydrate him caused only more vomiting, so I sent Rex ahead with Whitney and Dylan and asked him to buy the $39.99 remembrance video so I could relive swimming with the dolphins at home.

When the excursion was over, we boarded our returning safari bus and watched our fellow tourists gravitate to the opposite side and face the open window for the duration of the trip. Derek's skin was a yellowish gray. His eyes were red and sunk into the dark circles surrounding them. His breath smelled like acetone or cheap tequila. This was looking more serious to me than a typical case of enteritis, and I had decided to take him to a clinic for intravenous rehydration. However, on the way home Derek sat up and signed "pop" (American Sign Language for soda pop). Derek had some early language but by this time was virtually nonverbal. While everyone else proceeded to the pirate cruise, I rehabilitated Derek with Pepsi and saltine crackers. I was so relieved that his illness was brief. Soon he would be all better and perhaps even feeling well enough for … a moon dance.

When Derek proved to us that Montezuma's revenge was no mere threat, we all chugged Pepto-Bismol as a precaution, but Dylan and Rex still got mildly ill. Whitney lasted until the last day. She waited to board the plane home, lying on the cool tile floor of the airport, thinking only of the unbelievably giant cream puffs in a bakery window we passed, knowing she couldn't eat them. I never got sick. Rex said I'm too ornery for mere Mexican *E. coli.*

911—Breaking and Entering

I suddenly need a change of surroundings to interrupt the buzzing in my brain. I think I'll go see the people who live in the gray house at the end of the winding driveway. They usually give me crackers when I stand on their porch. I'd better hurry though. It's pretty cold, and if I'm gone very long, they'll come and get me. Mom wasn't finished pruning the tree branches and left the tools by the driveway. I choose one and notice how the coolness of the metal keeps my focus. I tap the blades on everything to hear the varying sounds and vibrations. I experience my environment using my "Derek-echolocation." The snow-covered ground is somehow soothing as I walk in my stocking feet. After a while I really don't feel anything. I wait awhile on the porch, but no one gives me anything to eat, so I walk around to the back of the house.

I see different faces looking at me out of the upstairs window, so I decide to go back home. I head up the hill to our long driveway. A green and white car is driving slowly behind me. A large man with a mustache like Dad's gets out and yells at me. He yells again, this time with an angry voice. He takes the tool away from me and shoves me hard against the car. He puts hard metal rings on my wrists and locks them behind my back. He puts me in the backseat of the car. There are a lot of cool gadgets that I would love to tap if I could. It is warm in the car, and my feet start to ache a little. The radio doesn't play music, and I don't understand the men's questions.

When we pull up to my house, one of the men gets out of the car and knocks on the front door. Mom won't hear it if she is still upstairs. He walks around to the back of the house, and pretty soon Mom comes running up to the car. I am glad her angry face isn't for me.

"911, what is the nature of your emergency?"

"Uh, yeah, there's a guy on my property with bolt cutters and he's trying to break into my storage shed. There's a foot of snow on the ground and he's barefoot—just socks. He must be on crack or something. He's around twenty years old, five foot nine, about 180 pounds, with short blonde hair. He's wearing black sweats and a white T-shirt.

When I walked downstairs, I was dumbfounded to find a sheriff's deputy standing on the back deck peering into the kitchen door window. A thousand thoughts raced through my mind: Are the kids okay? Is there a manhunt going on? Another cougar sighting? Derek? Where's Derek?

I tossed the folded clothes on the couch and opened the deck door. "May I help you?"

The deputy explained that the department had received a

report of a prowler from my neighbor and wanted to know if I had seen anything. He was holding my pruning shears. "Do you recognize these?"

When I responded that they were mine, he asked if I could identify the man they arrested. *Oh my god, they've arrested Derek and think he's a prowler!* I bolted off the deck to the front of the house and found Derek handcuffed in the back of a patrol car. He actually wasn't that upset; he seemed fascinated with all of the interesting equipment in the car and was merely ignoring the barrage of questions from the increasingly impatient young deputy. I was furious and amused at the same time.

"What in the hell are you doing with my son in your car? Take those handcuffs off immediately, or I'll own you and this whole county!" The older deputy informed me that Derek was under arrest for attempted breaking and entering.

I said, with hands on my hips and nostrils flaring, "He is a nonverbal, twelve-year-old autistic kid who has no idea what breaking and entering is."

"Then why was he found with bolt cutters on your neighbor's property?"

"They are not bolt cutters. I had been pruning trees on the driveway before it began to snow, and Derek must have picked the pruning shears up on the way to visit the neighbors. He doesn't know that the family who used to live there recently moved away."

When Derek noticed that I was becoming increasingly upset, he began to struggle against the cuffs. His expression had gone from calmly curious to anxious. I asked the older deputy to stop the situation from escalating any further and offered phone numbers for Derek's teacher and principal, along with his birth certificate. Derek looks like a typical twelve-year old; I had no idea why our new neighbor had mistaken him for an older grown man who was probably a drug addict.

The older deputy pulled Derek from the back of the car, removed the cuffs, and said they would calm the neighbors down and explain the circumstances. I wrote my name and number on a scrap of paper for the deputy to give to them in case Derek ever came calling again.

About fifteen minutes after the deputies left, the phone rang: my new neighbor, calling to apologize.

"I only called the police out of concern," he explained. "The child had no shoes on."

His explanation was quite a departure from the original 911 call that the officers described, but our new neighbors turned out to be a nice, older couple who were justifiably concerned. However, they had entirely misread Derek's intention and odd behavior, as is so often the case.

Later that afternoon the UPS man delivered a package from Amazon. In it was a book I had ordered titled *The Stress Reduction Handbook*. Perfect timing.

Chapter 2

MOTHER'S DAY

Last May, I asked for a special Mother's Day gift from Rex, Whitney, and Dylan. I wanted them each to write an essay titled "The Good, the Bad, and the Ugly of Derek's Autism." I asked for their most honest account of what it's been like having Derek in their lives. I was struck by how different the responses were, even given the age differences. One common theme did come through, though: we were all stronger, more resilient, and less superficial people because of Derek. I've included their writings so that other family members who are living with autism can relate to their accounts.

The first essay I received was from my daughter, Whitney. She is now twenty years old and is living in California as a college sophomore. She and Derek are only seventeen months apart, but their lives couldn't be any more different. Hers is filled with many accomplishments and vast possibilities. She is a champion runner, an accomplished harpist, and a valedictorian honor student with a black belt in karate. In contrast, Derek's world seems to shrink more every year, especially with the end of transition job training on the horizon. His escalations in aggressive behaviors further limits the time he is out in the community. He prefers to remain home, with no one requesting anything of him. I suppose we would all like that to some degree. I am currently struggling with how hard to push, pull, and prod Derek into a life larger than one that is comfortable for him.

I know that whatever direction Whitney's life takes, it will be rich and rewarding. I also know that she is a kind, sensitive soul who will look out for Derek when his battle-weary, old mom is no longer around. I have already prepared for Derek financially, so he will never be a financial burden on his brother or sister. Their only duty will be to check up on him occasionally to make sure he's safe and relatively happy. He'd probably also appreciate some Chinese takeout every now and then.

Dylan, my quirky fifteen-year-old, is one of those kids who doesn't fit well into any one group and yet is comfortable in all of them. He loves sports but hasn't quite found his niche yet. He is a lazy student who easily makes A's while always taking the path of least resistance. His lack of zeal in the classroom, however, is in stark contrast to his performance on the field, track, or mat, where he gives his all. Unfortunately, he inherited my own short stature. He might not be the biggest kid out there, but he is one of the toughest and with the most heart. He's kind of a computer nerd who likes to read cheesy sci-fi novels, and he entertains us with daily doses of malapropisms, such as "Dear dictionary, today I saw a moose."

Dylan

11

What struck me in his essay was how isolated he has been made to feel because of Derek. This is in spite of our concerted effort to make Whitney's and Dylan's lives as "normal" as possible. I was also moved by how reluctant Dylan was to even acknowledge the ugliness of Derek's autism. I am so proud of my children on so many levels.

Rex is my devoted husband of twenty years. When I tend to jump up and down in a crisis, he calmly and steadily puts one foot in front of the other toward a well-thought-out solution. I have made peace with Derek's autism and was somewhat surprised to read in Rex's essay that he really hasn't and probably never will. He is frustrated that he has to deal daily with a problem he can't fix. He would make a lousy guest on Oprah, as he is a man of few words who I have rarely seen emote. What he wrote for me was the only glimpse I've had into his true feelings about Derek—and I was somewhat taken aback to see unresolved despair and darkness. He usually writes me silly poems about the humor in our daily lives. His essay was a true departure from the norm.

Somewhere along the way, Rex and I struck a deal. Derek became "mine," and Dylan and Whitney became Rex's. He was the "good guy," and I was "the enforcer." I don't believe that we did this consciously, yet we did it nevertheless. I know that the ungodly hours Rex spent at the hospital working were in large part responsible for this. Rex spent most of his days off hauling Dylan and Whitney to sporting and social events so I didn't have to. It was just what worked for us. We don't always get to pick our roles in life; I know for sure that I didn't.

Whitney's Essay: Derek-the Good, the Bad, and the Ugly

Growing up with a brother with autism is a difficult experience to describe to others. When people ask about my siblings and I mention that my little brother has autism, reactions range from silence and pity to interest and excitement. Most people can't imagine what it is like to be connected to someone with autism, so they usually fall back on what they have seen in movies. The most common questions I get are "Is he a savant?" or "Is he a genius at math or something?" Most people don't realize that less than 1 percent of those with autism are savants.

I'm pretty sure Derek isn't a genius, but he definitely shows glimmers of intelligence. Mom says that he outsmarts her daily. He can be really sneaky and doesn't miss anything—especially when it comes to hidden goodies. I have to say, though, that the inner workings of his mind are truly a mystery to me. I would love to be able to be in his head for even a day to experience the world as he does. I'm unsure whether I view his condition with such normalcy because it has been a part of my life since I can remember or whether the reality of his condition is too painful to think about. We're only seventeen months apart, and when we were little, people used to think we were twins.

As long as I can remember, I have had a strong sense of guardianship over Derek. Early in our lives together, I didn't really understand why he couldn't talk and why he did weird things. Yet I knew I had to make sure everyone else knew not to expect normal behavior from him. I have a vivid memory of waiting with Derek for Mom in the dentist's office when I was about ten. A large woman came in with heavy makeup, big hair, and a long, colorful, flowing dress. Her perfume permeated the small waiting room.

She looked and smelled very huggable. Derek thought likewise and jumped up, ran across the room, and gave her a big hug. She was obviously shocked, so I dutifully ran after him and assured her, "It's okay, he's 'artistic,'" and led him away.

We actually still have this problem when we're out in public with Derek. He lunges at people, trying to get a better whiff of their cologne or deodorant. Once, he startled one woman at the mall so badly that she screamed and security was called. We always save the sample strips of perfume from fashion magazines to quickly hand to Derek; they distract him when someone approaches who has obviously overdone his or her odiferous application.

Another incident I remember is walking to lunch in fifth grade, when I heard screaming. I knew it was Derek, and I ran toward his classroom. He was throwing a major tantrum—kicking and screaming and writhing around on the hall floor. All of the classes were walking past him single file toward the cafeteria, and every single student turned and stared. I remember being really angry at all of them, even though their response was perfectly reasonable. I was crouching over Derek and yelling, "It's okay! Just keep walking!" I was always mildly embarrassed during these episodes, but I was more concerned that Derek was being judged for his behaviors.

The happiest times I have with Derek are when I tickle him; his laugh is so infectious. I like to see him smile and laugh because this is when he is most animated. I think I find these experiences most notable because on some level, I crave some emotional connection with him.

While growing up, I knew not to expect normal affection from Derek or even recognition that I was his sister, but I would sometimes become frustrated with this reality. I would wrap

Christmas presents for him just like the rest of my family and put a lot of thought into the gifts: "Well, he likes tapping things lately, so I should find the longest, most exciting tapper ever. He'll love it!" But because he had no concept of what a gift was, he didn't show the acknowledgment or appreciation I expected. Even though I now realize his limitations, I am still saddened by these memories. Derek doesn't get to have the simple pleasures so many of us take for granted. In the microcosm of our household, we have an equilibrium that mimics normalcy, and I tend to forget how differently we stack up to the rest of the world.

When my boyfriend came to visit my home last summer, he asked what he should do when meeting Derek. I had to say honestly that it really didn't matter—secretly praying that Derek wouldn't disrobe spontaneously or lunge toward him, trying to check out his aftershave. I'm also sad when I come home from college and he shows absolutely no excitement or even recognition.

Despite all of these truths, I somehow cannot believe that there isn't something more to him that we aren't giving him credit for. Recently, I heard that family members are encouraged to talk to stroke victims, even when the victims show no signs of recognition, because they understand on some level. I think that this is perhaps true for those with autism as well. When Derek looks at me blankly, I wonder if there really isn't someone inside praying that someone will understand him. When he has tantrums, we often attribute it to "teenage angst." But the anger I see from him is too extreme to be that simply defined. I believe a lot of his "anger" is really frustration and anxiety. There is so much more to him than is evident because of the shroud of autism. I sometimes catch myself using baby talk with him or being overly authoritarian, and I realize how I would feel if someone spoke that way to me. I think

I would have a similar reaction to his—especially considering the years and years of pent-up frustration he must have.

Derek's anger would sometimes be so intense that I would actually be afraid for my safety. It has caused our family many sleepless nights. I don't resent him for it, though. I wish there was some way we could alleviate his anxiety other than with medication, but right now that is all that works.

My mom does a good job of grounding Derek when he starts to lose control, but this means that she has to be with him at all times. In a way, it is good for him to have someone who is familiar with his emotions and knows how to help regulate them, but it is also a prison for them both.

It is great that Derek has begun to make advances in recognizing sight words and learning to use sign language to articulate his most basic needs. But most of all, I want him to be happy. Hopefully that will come from his increased communication abilities, as he can learn to be at peace with himself and those around him. Perhaps the most frustrating aspect of autism is feeling so close to reaching the person on either an intellectual or emotional level but never quite bridging the gap. An even sadder thought is that they probably feel the same way.

Dylan: The Good, the Bad, and the "No Ugly" of Derek

When Dad told me that Mom wanted me to write about the good, the bad, and the ugly about Derek for her Mother's Day gift, I thought to myself, "How the heck do I write about the ugly of Derek? That just doesn't compute." What is ugly, though, is the autism that has invaded his brain and our family. I cannot remember a single day when we have not been impacted somehow by Derek's autism. The effects can range from minor to really bad. Even our vacations are affected. For the last few years, Mom has stayed home with Derek because it's just not worth the potential for disaster.

The good about Derek is how he has made a huge change in how we think and act. I believe that Derek has actually made us better people. Due to his disability, he has made us look outside of ourselves and kept us from becoming selfish and small-minded. I feel guilty when I focus on something stupid and trivial. I get to know someone before jumping to conclusions about them. I wish more people would do that with Derek, rather than judging us harshly.

I also think our family is stronger because of Derek. We all look out for each other and are protective of Derek. I am proud when my mom says that I'm the only one she trusts with Derek. I don't have any problems when we're together, but I wish he was more able to shoot hoops and play computer with me like a normal brother. About the only word he says anymore is "pop pop" for popcorn, and I'm the one who got him to say it. So that's pretty cool.

The bad about Derek is how his condition has forced and

trained us to become somewhat antisocial. It's just an easier existence not having to worry about how people will react to Derek's often bizarre or frightening behaviors. We used to have a lot of parties and visitors, but not anymore.

About once a year I get to have a cool party with my friends from school, and Mom or Dad keep Derek busy so he won't do anything embarrassing. My best friend is used to Derek, and he comes over a lot on the weekends. It is also a strain going out with Derek because you never know what he'll do. He loves to eat and usually behaves at restaurants, but there's always a chance he'll just lose it for no apparent reason. I also don't think my parents, especially my mom, has as much energy for me because of the stress Derek causes. My parents have really tried to let my life be as normal as possible under the circumstances, but there is no denying the impact autism has made on all of our lives—especially Derek's.

Rex: The Good, the Bad, and the Ugly of Derek

Well, the good, the bad, and the ugly of Derek—quite an assignment. In thinking about it, I realize that all three qualities mix and that is what makes his/our situation so special/problematic. I hope I can explain—at least as I see it.

The Good

About the only good that comes out of Derek's autism is that it makes me take a step back and realize how silly and inconsequential are many of the things that other people seem so concerned about. Their issues seem so trivial that I want to smack them over the head and say, "If you think that's bad, try one weekend in my house, pal." People at work think I'm laid-back and nothing bothers me. Well, that's because in contrast to Derek, much of the rest of the problems in this life are really not worth much concern. So for that I guess I'm a better person. I just really don't "sweat the small stuff"—which is everything other than Derek.

When Derek is happy (making happy noises/smiling/looking at you with that goofy grin), not many things can bring you down. When he can be so happy with all that he has to contend with, I think to myself, "What do I have to complain about?" You know that his joy/happiness is real and not based on greedy materialism or encumbered by societal BS. Some people I work with may brag about a new sports car or a stock windfall, which seems to make them "happy," but with Derek, his happiness is real and so refreshing to see. When he's skipping down the driveway, laughing and tapping his golf club, a lot of the weight of the world is lifted from my shoulders.

But, here's the catch-22: a lot of that weight is Derek-related.

Am I thrilled for Derek's moments of bliss, or am I relieved because Derek is so occupied with his glee that I can have a moment not being on "alert mode"? That comes from living in the presence of Derek and that ability he has to escalate any situation into crisis mode. If I let my guard down for two seconds, Derek will be into some kind of mischief, or worse. The good, the bad, and the ugly of Derek seem to come at you from all directions at any given moment. My memories are flooded with crises we've had over the years.

Derek's wants and desires are painfully simple, and this is part of the "good of Derek." I can make him happier with a can of pop or an apple than with a thousand-dollar laptop. He has no desire for anything materialistic. He responds more to simple praise— even just a smile—than anything else (well, that isn't food).

The Bad

Well, where to start?

Obsessive-compulsive behaviors (which he probably inherited from me). Thankfully, new medications have come out that have really improved this situation. His behavior is still maddening, but nothing like it would have been without the medications he now takes. I will be looking for something important on my desk and after a couple of minutes realize that Derek has struck again. I wonder how much time we have all spent searching for Derek-appropriated items. At least they're usually found crammed behind the desk or bookcase, maybe in the heater duct. The OCD behaviors make Derek fairly predictable, as he is pretty consistent in his intent. After putting Derek on meds, we now actually have utensils in drawers rather than in any other conceivable or unimaginable locations.

After way too many years of sleepless nights, it became

abundantly clear that Derek would need to be locked in his bedroom at night; roaming around in the woods at 2 AM or consuming an entire jar of coffee crystals in the pantry was no longer an option. If anyone has a problem with that, they're welcome to camp out at his door all night like my wife used to do. In reality, Derek seems to enjoy being in his secure and quiet room. We have placed a portable toilet in there for use during the night, and the less-than-pleasant duty of emptying it has somehow fallen to me. But in my mind, it absolves me from the ways I may fall short in the day-to-day care and handling of Derek.

Another challenge with Derek is conflicts. When he escalates to the point of aggression, there is really no way to handle him without being physical. This is very uncomfortable for me. I know that I am only trying to restrain him for his own safety, but it is an ugly scene. I remember one time when he really went off in a restaurant parking lot (I still don't know why), and I was worried that someone might call the police. He now outweighs me, and I have had to increase the necessary force required to contain him when he becomes aggressive. I know Derek can't help losing control sometimes and shouldn't be punished for it. I would just rather avoid these situations. My wife is out and about with him all during the week, and I really don't know how she does it. She is literally half his size and controls him better that anyone.

Men like to be able to take a situation or problem and fix it. Solutions are not very forthcoming with Derek, and it is frustrating to not know what to do. A trip to Disney World was ruined when Derek was about three or four. One night in the hotel room, he screamed and wailed inconsolably and inexplicably. I was afraid that someone might call security. I put Derek in the car, and we drove around and around the parking lot of the complex most of the night, as this seemed to be the only thing that would calm him.

Finally, he fell asleep at about 5:00 AM, too exhausted to cry any more, and I carried him back to the room. We still do not know what was wrong and certainly didn't know how to fix it then. He probably just wanted to be in his own bed at home instead of in a pricey Disney hotel three thousand miles away. The only part of the trip he did like was the actual plane flight and the pop and peanuts he received on it.

The Ugly

Truly, the ugliest part of this whole picture was the diagnosis sixteen years ago and the implications of that diagnosis. Because while in training to become a physician, I had dealt with autistic children in medical school, I felt as though Derek had died. All of the hopes and aspirations you have for your child vanish in an instant. You experience numbness, detachment, and loss—gut-wrenching loss. Your son has "died," and yet there is still this little alien before you that you don't even know. The day after he was diagnosed, I can remember sitting in my office in a complete fog, totally oblivious to my surroundings as the life-changing ramifications of autism settled in. I was plunged into Conrad's *Heart of Darkness*, me as Marlow trying to rescue my son, Derek from the autism void, only to have him die in the end. Sometimes the ugliest part of the whole deal is what we do or what goes through us in response to Derek or the situation Derek puts us in. Love and a sense of humor help keep the darkness at bay. The fact that I can't outthink or solve the riddle of autism leaves me feeling impotent and empty.

In contrast to Derek, I am able to help my other kids. I can take Dylan to the batting cages to improve his batting average. I can help him with his math homework and give him advice. I taught Whitney to drive, advised her on running, and helped her with chemistry and physics. These are the tangibles that are gratifying to parents—tangibles that don't exist with Derek. Derek is considered low-functioning (needing help with nearly all aspects of daily living) and is nonverbal. He doesn't like to play games, and he has little receptive language; there really aren't a lot of ways to relate to him. He has associated me with food treats. I am inevitably met with requests for pop or cookies. He has always liked to ride in the car, and one of our best times was a road trip that just Derek and I recently took, which included dinners at greasy spoons and staying at various motels along the way. It was just an eight hundred mile circle, a trip to nowhere. He was so happy during that trip that he was med-free for three days. The only unhappiness shown was when we were returning from the trip. We turned onto the familiar street leading home, and Derek recognized that his trip was over. He reached over and tried to slam the gearshift into park (I never would have guessed that he knew the function of the transmission).

When Derek was about four, we were at a barbecue; and a partner asked why my son was eating dirt. I told him that Derek had autism and explained some of what my partner had not learned in medical school. I then told him that I would gladly cut off my right arm if Derek could somehow be normal—not a star athlete, not a Nobel Prize–winner—just a normal kid. That offer still stands.

There is no ugliness in Derek, but the monster—autism—is ugly and cruel.

* * *

This is a copy of the one and only Christmas letter I sent out about ten years ago. It's a pretty good snapshot of what daily life can be like for the Porter family.

An Ode to December

It's been quite a year, though there's been worse,
But this month of December has come with a curse.
Lucky, our dog's name will have to be changed,
Since his hindquarters have been seriously rearranged.
When he chased the UPS truck, he should have zigged and not zagged,
Now, his fluffy tail no longer shall wag.
Says the vet:
"We'll just flip this flap here and flop this flap there—
Who cares if he won't have any skin or hair.
And when the flaps rot, no cause for excitation,
We'll rely at this point on pure granulation."
So ole Lucky's butt is infected and bloating,
And when the washer overflowed on soapsuds he was floating.
He didn't seem to mind this unexpected bidet,
though he prefers to take baths in the usual way.
Retrospectively, I should have obeyed my first instinct—
A ballsy gal pal with a .38 made of zinc.
But she just couldn't do it, and neither could I.
So she picked Lucky up and plopped him in the van with a sigh.
After three surgeries and at least two more to go,
The fate of poor Lucky, we just do not know.
On my way home with all of the kids,
Our steep, icy road caused all cars to skid.
When all of a sudden, there arose such a clatter,
Mom yelled, "Duck your heads, or your brains will be splattered."
Daddy rounded the last curve just as we did,
But his trusty old jeep went into a skid.
No toooo much damage, and we all are okay,

Just the perfect end to a not-so-perfect day.
Whitney's teacher hates her; Dylan has one that he loves.
Derek's Michele was sent from above.
Derek likes to be naked and needs doses of Beano;
Are we experiencing karma or maybe El Niño?
I'm in an investment club called On the Rise.
Some are doing better since taking SSRIs.
Daddy's job is a pain; most of the partners are okay.
Maybe Fred will move to Timbuktu and make everybody's day.
We're determined to be positive and resolute,
And to our dear friends who support us, a hearty solute.
We're healthy (except Lucky), happy, and surrounded with love,
All the crap we've endured, we'll just rise above.
No doubt about it, this month's been a killer;
I can't kick my dog, so I'll just fax Dick Miller.

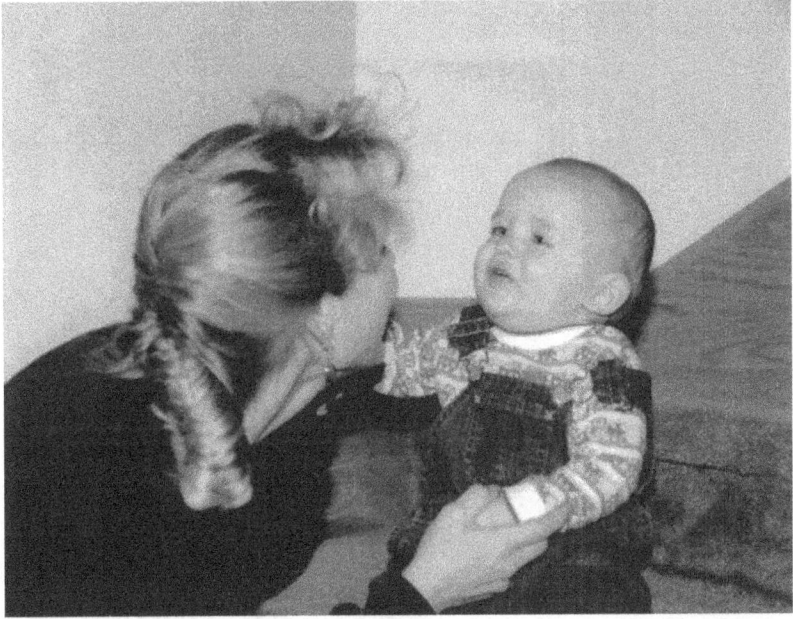

Derek at three months with Mom

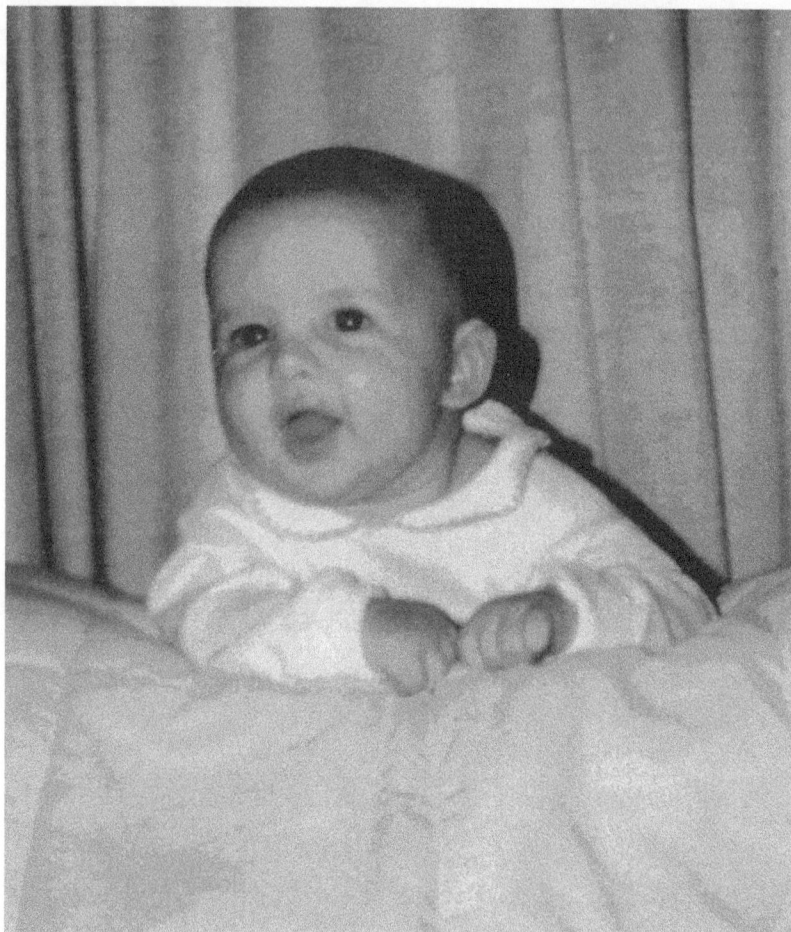

Derek at one month

Derek, age four, at New Smyrna Beach, Florida

Derek at age three

Derek at age two

Derek at age seventeen

Chapter 3

DEREK

My life with Derek is difficult, stressful, and exhausting. It is also, however, rich, rewarding, and definitely not boring.

Derek began life as a cute, perfectly normal-appearing infant. When Derek was about a month old, I remember a stranger commenting that my child resembled Dick Butkus. I, however, thought Derek grew into a gorgeous toddler, with a head full of honey-blond hair and dreamy blue eyes.

The first concern I had about Derek was that he was too good. He slept through the night as soon as we came home from the hospital. This was in stark contrast to my experience with Whitney, who rarely slept through the night for her first year. I would have to set an alarm during the night for Derek's feedings.

My second concern about Derek came when he was about six months. He would avert his eyes from mine when I held him and attempted to interact with him. This worried me to the core, as I remembered how Whitney constantly stared into my eyes with love and fascination. Six years before Derek was born, I was in nursing school. During my psychiatric rotation, I spent a week in a pediatric ward for children with autism. I distinctly remembered "the faraway eyes" of so many of the children there. They had a very difficult time making eye contact. When I expressed my concerns about Derek to friends and family, they brushed them aside or discounted them outright. I knew something wasn't right but wasn't ready to consider autism at that point.

At Derek's one-year checkup, I discussed with his pediatrician the worrisome symptoms and developmental deficits, such as absence of imitation, pointing, and appropriate play. The pediatrician was very dismissive, explaining that language is often delayed in males, and he pointed out that Derek had hit most of his developmental milestones, like sitting up, crawling, walking, and early speech. He added that I should not expect every child to be as precocious and bright as Whitney. I was condescendingly reassured and told not to worry.

My friend Pule recently recalled that when our families were together at the beach, and I caught a large fish. Everyone was so excited—except for Derek, who was two at the time. Rex had him on his shoulders, and Derek was mesmerized by the sand that stuck to his hands, oblivious to the commotion around him. It was at that moment that Pule believed that the concerns I had shared with her about Derek were valid.

As a toddler, Derek was an extremely picky eater, so I had to supplement his diet with protein and vitamins. I hated holding him down while he screamed, trying to get a small protein shake down his throat by using a turkey baster. Then, the only food he was interested in was French fries. If we tried to pass the golden arches without stopping to get him some fries, he would scream until we did.

At the age of two, my concerns solidified, and my resolve to get some real answers was steeled. By his second birthday, Derek had about a twenty-word vocabulary, could count to ten, and could say the alphabet. Even though he could articulate words, his tone sounded like that of a deaf child. I tested his hearing by crinkling candy wrappers out of view. With 100 percent accuracy, Derek would locate and consume the candy. My method didn't satisfy the professionals whose advice I sought, so I scheduled a hearing test with an audiologist. It was a complete disaster. Derek screamed the entire time and threw the headphones across the room each time the audiologist placed them on his little head. I still don't know how the audiologist was able to conclude anything with Derek's lack of cooperation. I think *everyone* was just glad to be done.

It seemed as though a curtain had come down overnight, separating Derek from his familiar world. He lost all of his language and gestures. (It is a common occurrence for children with infantile autism to lose their language at about the age of two.) He began playing obsessively and inappropriately with strange, inanimate objects. For example, he became inexorably attached to a plastic spatula, while his pile of toys sat untouched. If he picked up a toy car, he would turn it upside down and spin the wheels, never racing it around like a typical child would. Words appeared briefly, among much jabbering and jargon, and then disappeared altogether. After age two, his words were never an attempt to communicate but rather a singsong way of entertaining himself. His only interaction with anyone was to pull them to something he wanted.

Derek was in his own little world and would scream inconsolably when I tried so desperately to bring him back to us by interrupting his inappropriate rituals and trances. I would insert myself into whatever self-stimulating activity he was engaged in and mirror his actions. His lack of eye contact was marked, despite my efforts to get on the floor with him at his level and establish a connection. I knew for certain that he was autistic. He had become one of those little lost souls that I'd seen in the pediatric psych ward. I can remember being struck by how little their mothers meant to those children. The mothers were mere tools to be used motorically, like forceps used to obtain a desired object that is out of reach; they could just as well have been complete strangers. I felt so horrible for those poor young mothers, absolutely irrelevant to their children. Now I was one of them. When my daughter was little, I knew how exhaustingly and persistently I was needed and wanted. The contrast with Derek was heartbreaking.

He was almost three when the pediatrician stopped treating me like a neurotic nutcase and scheduled Derek for a very difficult battery of tests. Everything was normal, except Derek.

We were sent to a speech therapist, who made absolutely no headway. I changed doctors again and made an appointment with a new pediatrician who had a reputation for diagnosing developmental disabilities. The appointment lasted about ten minutes. She asked me some questions and observed Derek for a short period, during which he was totally preoccupied with my checkbook. I wanted to take it from him and encourage him to interact appropriately when I saw the knowing recognition register on her face. I hated that she knew what I was dreading to hear. I fought back the tears that were beginning to well. She did no examinations or tests. She simply told me that Derek was autistic and handed me a copied stack of articles from various journals.

I was relieved and nauseated at the same time. The diagnosis I feared at least gave me some direction. I don't remember driving home. I held it together until I had to tell Rex, who was in total denial. He didn't say a word—just held me until I was too exhausted to sob any more. We spent the next years mourning our little boy, who hadn't died but was "gone" just the same. Derek's profound withdraw lasted about two years. He wandered around in a daze, tapping his favorite plastic screwdriver on whatever he passed, always seeming to be on a secret mission that to anyone else would seem pointless. It was as if he were trying to divine something or search for meaning in the different resonations of various materials he tapped.

The grip of autism seemed to lessen at about age four or five. The curtain that had descended and separated us turned from heavy brocade to translucent voile. Derek became a lot more animated and social, and he gradually became a part of us again. The first eye contact he made was a sly, knowing, little sideways glance. It was wonderful to see him smile and giggle with delight when we pushed him in his swing. I don't attribute these changes to anything in particular, but now that I've studied research on autistic brain development, I think it was partly developmental—his brain was somehow adjusting to its deficits. Maybe secondary circuitry was forming; maybe he knew that we weren't going to give up on him.

School Age

A major accomplishment we made with Derek was potty training. When he was about to turn six years old, Derek still showed no interest in independent toileting. Before he started the first grade, I made up my mind that we were just going to get it done. I waited for a weekend when my husband was going to be home and informed everyone that I was unavailable until further notice. I got a sleeping bag, a pillow, all of Derek's favorite foods and drinks, the fattest novel I could find, and no diapers. I locked us in the bathroom and installed the potty seat, and there we stayed. I read, and he ate and drank … for hours. With a lot of coaxing and a little help with aim, success with number one came fairly easily. Number two didn't happen for about another eighteen hours. We did not leave the bathroom once for the entire weekend, but when we emerged potty trained, everyone rejoiced. We ceremoniously threw the diapers in the trash, donned big-boy briefs, and headed to China Buffet to celebrate.

Friends refer to my method as the Porter Potty Party Plan. It is really just about clarifying the expectations and limiting the options that are available to only those that are desired. It is also important to keep the experience positive by using favorite treats, drinks, and fun.

I was so fixated about potty training Derek that it didn't even occur to me that Dylan, at age three, should also be trained. When he started nursery school, I told him that he was a big boy now and wouldn't be wearing diapers anymore. He said, "Okay, Mom," and that was it.

A chilling memory I have of Derek was right around this time, at age five or six. Any discernable language had long disappeared; he still jabbered, but it was self-entertaining sound-play, with an occasional recognizable word. We were in the kitchen preparing an afternoon snack. He looked up at the clock on the oven and said, as plain as day, "It's time to get Whitney" —and it was. He not only spoke in a coherent, appropriate sentence; he also told time and showed acute awareness of our routine. I was nonplussed. I grabbed him and said, "Say it again!" In an instant, his bright recognition was replaced with the usual dreamy countenance. He had allowed me just a glimpse, but it was enough to let me know that he was still here.

Derek attended preschool (ages three and four), kindergarten (age five), and first grade (age six), while mainstreamed at the public early-education center in our district. When Dylan was old enough to attend preschool there, I became Derek's one-on-one aide, accompanying him to school every day during kindergarten and first grade. From the ages of seven through seventeen, we enrolled Derek in a special-education, self-contained classroom at our district elementary school.

When Derek was ten, he participated in the Special Olympics. His elementary school teacher, Michele, was the coach for the district and really encouraged his involvement. The truth is that Derek probably could not have cared less about the event. I would literally have to drag him through his practices. Ironically, he medaled in the district meets and qualified for state in the softball throw and one of the running events. When he was awarded his medals on the podium, he looked down at them, smelled them to see if they were edible, and flung them over a fence. He experienced none of the pride that his fellow champions felt. He did, however, enjoy the road trip across state, which meant staying in a motel and eating out.

Even when Derek was little, it was difficult to keep baby-sitters. When Derek was five, we took the kids to Disney World. We met with some friends for dinner and left the children with our friends' nanny. If cell phones had been common back then so that she could have called us when she had a problem, I doubt she would have lasted ten minutes. When we returned, Derek was screaming at the top of his lungs, Whitney and Dylan were upset, and the nanny looked visibly ill. She was in such a hurry to leave that she walked out without being paid.

At about age eleven, Derek began puberty. His behaviors became more inappropriate and unpredictable, and he became harder to control. At this point, Derek divided our family into two teams that I continue to refer to as A and B. The A team consists of Rex, Whitney, and Dylan. Derek and I are the B team. Rarely are both teams in the game at the same time. Sometimes we tag team, but usually the A team does the traveling, the sporting events, or the social gatherings of any kind. I am so beyond embarrassment that Derek's inappropriate antics really aren't the reason we don't do a lot of things as a family; it is just that no one can enjoy an outing when there's the tension of knowing that Derek is likely going to ruin the experience with a meltdown.

It is not really an issue now that the kids are older, but there have been times when I've resented missing out on special moments in my other children's lives. I missed Dylan's first touchdown and his winning first place in the science fair. Derek was having an especially bad day when Whitney had her Mother's Day harp concert, so I wasn't there when she played *Scheherazade* for me. I think I've been to one of Rex's office holiday parties in the last ten years. Either he goes alone, or we don't go at all. We have no family in the area, and Derek is now too old, large, and difficult to stay with the average teenage sitter. We could hire someone to stay with Derek, but he can quickly size up who is unwilling or unable to impose order when he has an angry outburst; and he is very opportunistic in this regard. The lack of respite care in our area means that we usually use it only in emergency circumstances. Moreover, because of some negative past experiences, I am uncomfortable with strangers in my home, especially since Derek is unable to communicate any mistreatment.

The way it stands now is that the only person we leave Derek with for an occasional quick dinner out is his brother, Dylan. They usually pop in a DVD and watch it together with a big bowl of popcorn. Dylan is patient with Derek, and Derek knows that Dylan isn't going to demand anything from him or cause him any anxiety. They actually get along quite well.

As for family vacations, the complicated lives of a busy high school jock and a college coed have made scheduling increasingly difficult. But when trips are possible, Derek and I stay home with the animals and garden. We would love to be near the ocean again, but the hassles and potential for disaster make it not worth the trip. I could easily live with the disapproving glares but not flights being aborted because of a screaming, thrashing Derek. Derek might do just fine with appropriate medication, but the stakes are a lot higher now because of his large size and potential aggression—and I'm a lot older.

Derek is now eighteen, an adult who is totally dependent on us. He is in a job-training transition program based at his high school. There, he does tasks such as sweeping the gym and transferring recycled paper to the appropriate bins. He is also part of a maintenance crew that picks up trash at the schools in our district. We are in the process of finding him supported employment in the community. There are agencies that contract work with local companies and supervise and support workers so that they can be successfully employed, but Derek still has serious behavior problems that have to be continually addressed and curtailed. He is on medications for anxiety and aggression, which have really helped make him a happier kid.

Derek is not a savant. I'm pretty sure he's smart by the way he outsmarts me daily, but he tests very low, cognitively. He is nonverbal and difficult to test. He won't be able to attend college. We haven't cured or overcome Derek's autism, but we have had many successes, large and small, as a truly happy family.

When I asked my husband for five adjectives to describe Derek, he gave the following: *demanding, unpredictable, enigmatic, explosive,* and *elusive.* The five I came up with are *engaging, frustrated, predictable, obsessive,* and *simplistic.* I was struck by the subjective differences in the impressions of our son.

Objectively, Derek is a handsome man/boy; he appears normal at first, but at second glance, most people are aware that something is not quite right. It might be an odd facial expression, a weird gaze, or an inappropriate mannerism, such as sucking his thumb. He might make an undistinguishable utterance or scowl angrily. He'll skip gleefully in bursts for no apparent reason. He generally ignores people he doesn't know, but if he is comfortable with you, he'll engage you by standing in front of you and looking you directly in the eyes. Those who are unfamiliar with Derek may find this disconcerting. This intense eye contact is in stark contrast to that of the three-year-old who wouldn't make eye contact for anything or anyone. He is receptive when kids at his school engage him, but he never initiates these interactions. Most personnel at school approach him with peace offerings in the form of sweet treats. Derek has grown in so many areas, but he still faces seemingly insurmountable challenges.

One of his most unlikely characteristics for one with autism is the existence of empathy. Derek has always been in tune with the moods of others, and someone else's anxiety soon becomes his own. He easily picks up on any tension in a room and gets upset when kids cry—and not because of the noise. His beloved teacher once tripped while out on the playground and really went down, skinning her knee. Derek ran over to her, pulled her up, and helped her, all the way back to the classroom. Everyone just watched in amazement at this unexpected reaction. They might have expected him to become anxious or agitated but not to offer tender aid and assistance. When he was little, he probably would not have even noticed what happened.

Derek is not able to ride a bike but, weather permitting, he will occasionally ride his "chariot," a sort of double skateboard with handlebars. There's not much that Derek truly likes to do. In the summer, he spends a lot of time wandering around the yard, tapping a golf club or other such implement along the ground or anything he comes across. He explores his world by obsessively tapping an object on anything he passes. Derek's high school class recently went on a field trip to the local museum and absolutely drove the security guard crazy. The guard must have told Derek twenty times that he wasn't allowed to touch anything, and every time Derek ignored him, happily tapping everything in sight. We finally headed to the snack bar when it looked as though the security guard could take no more.

Derek is most happy in the pool. I have a love/hate relationship with our pool, as it is a pain to maintain and yet is an invaluable therapeutic tool for Derek. During the summer he spends most of his days serenely floating in the warm water. He often jumps up and down in the shallow end while "singing" exuberantly. He's no Pavarotti, but when he makes his repetitive rhythmic vocalizations that we refer to as song, it is a sign of contentment and happiness. For that reason, and that reason only, it is music to our ears.

Derek's medication needs usually fluctuate on a day-to-day basis, depending on the stressors, anxiety-inducing activities, and other factors he must deal with. When the levels are inadequate, he exhibits more obsessive-compulsive tendencies and is more likely to become angry or agitated. In the pool, when he hasn't had adequate medication, he compulsively swims around the periphery, splashing water on the dry cement deck to keep it wet. By the time he has completely covered the pool's edge, the sun has dried it and he must begin again. When Derek is in a calmer mood, he floats like a manatee in the deep end, where it is more shaded. I was a nervous wreck when he first ventured over into the deep end. Even though he had demonstrated his ability to "swim" in the deeper water, I would anxiously watch him from the window, happily bobbing with only his nose breaking the surface of the water for air. He has developed a unique swimming form that works well for him, and I no longer worry about his safety in the water.

If Derek catches my eye while I'm at the kitchen window, he'll sign "apple" to me, and I'll throw him one from the open window to perfect his day. It has become a summer tradition, so I have to keep the pantry stocked with apples. He used to ask for other things, but most don't float as well as apples.

In the winter when the pool is closed, he'll take several baths a day and will constantly request snacks and pop. He'll occasionally leaf through a book without reading it. He used to have favorite videos that he would watch over and over, but for a while he seemed to have outgrown them, choosing instead the Food Network. Recently, however, he resurrected some old Disney tapes that he has been watching repeatedly; *Aladdin* is his current favorite. I ordered them on DVD so we wouldn't have to keep rewinding them, but he stridently resisted when I first tried to play them. It took him a few weeks to accept the newer versions. It's that whole resistance to change and need-for-sameness thing. Derek has one computer game at school that he attends to somewhat, but he really has no interest in video games. He used to love to ride horses when he was little, but he's developed a fear of them, although I can't remember anything traumatic happening that would explain the change. He tolerates the many pets in our home but never initiates any interaction with them. One of our cats that is particularly friendly often sits by or on Derek, and he awkwardly pets her with a heavy hand. Dogs that jump on him or lick him cause him anxiety.

Many of Derek's annoying obsessive behaviors have abated since he's been given medication for anxiety and OCD. Before, we would never have silverware in the drawer because he'd put it down the heater ducts. If something came up missing, you could be pretty sure that Derek had crammed it somewhere, often behind my husband's heavy rolltop desk. Thankfully, Derek has also given up on another of his old compulsions: public nudity. The UPS man is especially grateful for this. When the weather cooperated, Derek used to run outside, take off all of his clothes, and throw them on the roof.

We were at a Fourth of July party at the home of one of Rex's partners when Derek was six. One of the guests discreetly informed us that Derek was in the kitchen, playing with water in the sink and not wearing any clothes. At some point, perhaps here, the reader must wonder: Why on earth don't they keep a better eye on Derek when they clearly know the mischief that he is capable of? The truth is that Derek has uncanny perception and will patiently wait for the opportunity to carry out his well-planned missions. Despite scoring low cognitively, I have always suspected a high intellect because of his intuitiveness. I consider myself to be a hyper-vigilant parent, and yet Derek has been able to pull off some pretty sophisticated skullduggery over the years. He does this by behaving for periods long enough to lull us into a false sense of security, and we let our guard down. Although one might think that he isn't even paying attention, he doesn't miss a trick. I believe most of the mischief Derek gets into is mostly from a lack of constructive activities he is able to do.

Recently, we decided to rebuild our rotting deck. I was given the task of staining the support beams, which are long and heavy. Derek was a huge help, carrying the boards to be painted and stacking them once they were dry. He really enjoys being helpful when he understands what is asked of him, and he beams with pride at his infrequent successes. I'm constantly wracking my brain, trying to find ways in which he can truly be helpful.

Sadly, Derek's only real passion is food. He'll eat just about anything, except cheese and eggs. When he was little, he even ate an occasional stinkbug; fortunately, that predilection was short-lived. About the time he began puberty, Derek transformed from the pickiest eater on the planet to someone who eats with true gusto. He likes strong pungent tastes like onions, garlic, and chilies. If I'd let him, he would drink an entire bottle of Worcestershire sauce. Once I found him with an empty jar of instant coffee crystals that had been full the day before. I don't dare have any coffee with caffeine in the house because there is a real danger that he would overdose on it. Even if the coffee were under lock and key, Derek would find a way to get it. He loves ethnic foods, possibly because of all of the different spices. We usually spend money that he receives as gifts at Thai or Indian restaurants.

Derek's sanctuary is his darkened basement bedroom; he retreats there when there is more in his world than he can contend with. Some days, we have to coax him out with promises of favorite foods and activities; other times he chooses to stay there most of the day. This latter action has become a sign that it might be time to adjust Derek's medication dosage. When we force Derek to venture out on days that he would rather not, he insists on wearing his pilled and worn gray hooded sweatshirt, which serves as his shroud. Since it replaced his threadbare security blanket from preschool years, Derek wears such a sweatshirt until the very last day of school, when temperatures were well into the nineties. Because of the security he feels the sweatshirt affords him, I can only willingly get him to take it off with the bribe of a Slurpee. I'm sure that the old country song "Make the World Go Away" would be Derek's soundtrack if he could understand the words and it had a better beat.

Derek has rarely shown any interest in music, but the other day we were riding in the car after picking up Dylan from school. While enduring my somewhat dated but (I believe) good taste in music, Derek became especially animated when the Doors' "Break On Through" began to play. He laughed and seat-danced to the entire song. As we all bobbed up and down to the beat of the music, the whole car bounced. Every time I play that song now, Derek rocks out. He couldn't possibly know the title of the song or the incredible significance it has with his disorder, but it is now Derek's official theme song ... and so, the title of this book.

Chapter 4
HOLIDAYS

I've always been a huge traditionalist when it comes to the holidays and used to go all out when the kids were younger. Over the years Derek has been "trained" to participate in our celebrations in his own way, but he doesn't really understand the traditions or the meaning behind them. He is usually compliant because he equates holidays with food. He will now open gifts he is handed, but he will generally toss them aside because most material items are unimportant to him. At Christmas, he prefers his stocking to the presents because he has learned that it contains favorite treats, which he prefers to the ubiquitous electronics gifts. Thanksgiving is probably his favorite holiday because it is not as frantic or distracting, and it revolves around huge quantities of food. Turkey drumsticks and green beans drenched in Worcestershire sauce are two of his favorites.

During Easter, we finally got him to participate in the Easter egg hunt by teaching him that the plastic eggs had candy inside. My other kids much preferred the eggs stuffed with money. There would always be a golden egg containing a ten-dollar bill. If Derek found it, he would toss it aside and continue hunting for the good stuff. He has no concept of money and doesn't understand that he could use it to purchase whatever treat he wanted. I doubt that we could motivate him to participate in any celebration that didn't somehow involve food.

Since about the age of six or seven, Derek has blown out

candles on his birthday cake, although I'm sure he doesn't know to "make a wish." He has, however, figured out that after he blows out the candles, he gets to eat cake and ice cream while saying "yum yum yum." He has a huge sweet tooth, but I have to monitor the sweets and junk food he eats; he has a tendency to gain weight, and his medication puts him at risk of metabolic syndrome. (Some of the atypical antipsychotic medications that are given to those with autism to control agitation and aggression have risk factors that include this syndrome, characterized by weight gain, increased triglycerides, elevated blood pressure, insulin resistance, and increased clotting factors in the blood. Metabolic syndrome can lead to diabetes and arterial plaque buildup, increasing the risk of heart and kidney disease and stroke.)

Derek doesn't have a clue about Valentine's Day, but he thoroughly enjoyed the goody bag of treats he used to receive at school. The whole Porter family used to go all out for Halloween. We would turn the basement into a "haunted house" and fully decorate the front yard. We have had several costume parties, and Derek was usually a pretty good sport about tolerating his costumes. Two costumes that I can remember his seeming to enjoy were Elvis and Bob Marley. Derek loved the reward of candy from trick-or-treating, but he never understood the concept of it. The last year that Rex took all three kids trick-or-treating, Derek tried to enter the first home that they went to. It probably just made more sense to him to take refuge from the cold night in the warm, cozy home, although it bewildered the owners. He became agitated when Rex carried him back out to the car. So, during subsequent years, Derek and I chose to stay home and watch *It's the Great Pumpkin, Charlie Brown*, while Whitney and Dylan hit a few extra houses to share their haul with him when they got home.

Chapter 5
ONWARD AND UPWARD

After Derek was diagnosed, I insatiably read everything on autism in print and organized all the material into different piles. I immediately discarded information that was purely anecdotal and unfounded. I filed one pile away for future reference, and designated the "active" pile for information to further research. This last included several recommended educational programs, various and sundry therapies, and articles on people of all kind of backgrounds specializing in autism. I don't even know how many thousands of dollars we spent on therapy that simply did not work. The only thing I remember getting out of those months of expensive therapy is head lice. I discovered to my horror that in one waiting room, the furniture was crawling with them. I looked down at newborn Dylan and noticed small "spots" creeping up his tiny yellow sleeper. I stripped it off of him and left it there. I wrapped him in a blanket, grabbed Derek, and couldn't get home quickly enough to get us deloused.

I made appointments with professionals from all over whose work impressed me. Most provided me with many useful strategies and ideas to try with Derek. (I will describe these further in chapter 22.) I visited many programs across the country that were showing promising results. Until Derek was three, we had to drive across state to the University of Washington for early intervention therapy with Dr. Geraldine Dawson and her staff; at the time, the area we lived in was a virtual black hole of resources. There, I would take

Derek to therapists and end up lending them my books because they didn't know anything about autism. Despite my misgivings, which were based only on my instincts and the fact that Derek was the only child there with autism, I put him in a program for children with developmental disabilities—virtually the only such program in Spokane. One day while we were there, Derek fell and hit his head hard enough for a large knot to form. I asked the teacher for some ice and was told not to worry because "autistics don't feel pain." After a few choice words to this person, we left and didn't go back.

Derek then started Millwood preschool in our local district. It was a cheerful building full of warm, well-intentioned people, but Derek was the first child they knew with autism. However, we were all willing to learn, and we took classes together, attended seminars, and consulted with experts as needed. He was there for almost four years, including two years of preschool, kindergarten at age five, and first grade at age six.

During this period at the Millwood Early Child Education Center, Derek's teachers consulted his school psychologist, Jill Madsen, daily to intervene and work her magic when Derek's tantrums escalated. Jill wrote the crisis response, a modified version of which is still in place for Derek's aggressive episodes. Through the years she has been an invaluable friend and advocate. When Derek was having an awful time adjusting to high school, she reminded me again that the important thing was whatever was best for Derek, not whatever was efficacious for the school. At times, when I became weary, she was there with her gentle strength to champion me in advocating for Derek. She told me that the course of her professional path was set when she met Derek.

Jill is now in private practice and has moved into a beautifully renovated Victorian home that is now her office. Derek and I recently attended her fancy opening, where I realized that Derek had touched many of the lives of those who attended. As familiar faces from the past kept appearing, it was like Derek's "six degrees of separation." One of Jill's partners was Derek's behavior therapist fifteen years ago. His preschool teacher when he was three was there and is now the vice principal at his high school. Jill's husband, Dan, was the principal at Millwood when Derek was there. Her son, Kyle, was in first grade with Derek. Barb and Nancy were Derek's occupational therapist and speech therapist, respectively. Karen was the physical therapist at Millwood. Some people I didn't even recognize said they knew Derek. All of these special people have greatly impacted us at various stages of Derek's growth and development. Derek congenially positioned himself in the center of the room, near the expansive array or hors d'oeuvres. Like the hub of a wheel, the guests seemed to encircle him at the periphery. I felt such a sense of community.

Sir Derek of Millwood

His dreamy eyes are sparkling blue

Yet show no sign of what's getting through.

He's a joy to us; an enigma to all,

Each gain is great and yet so small.

His greatest loves are horses, the sink, and his dad.

When we forget his blanket, it makes us all sad.

When free in the gym, you'd better steer clear,

No holds barred, no restraints, no fear!

His picture exchange worked for a while,

Now he plucks them all off, and they sit in a pile.

He subsists on gummy bears, pretzels, and flowers,

And bathwater from the tub where he'll stay for hours.

With the help of Nancy, Jill, and Dee,

Somehow he'll become the best he can be.

He warms the hearts of all those he meets,

Even his siblings think that he's neat.

We take one step forward and three steps back,

But just one of his smiles keeps me on track

Constance Porter

1992

Chapter 6

SETH WOODARD ELEMENTARY SCHOOL

When Derek was seven, he "graduated" from preschool and began what would become the next twelve years with his new teacher. My first impression of his new classroom was not that favorable. Derek was to be in a self-contained classroom of children with a wide range of disabilities. At the time he started, he would be the only child with autism. When we first visited to get a feel for his new program, I remember seeing a cute girl with severe cerebral palsy sitting in a far corner facing the wall. She was being informed that a "sad face" would remain by her name on the behavior chart until she decided to participate in the assigned activity, as all of the students were expected to do. I thought to myself, *Yikes, these people are so mean.* If there had been any other option for Derek at that time, I'm sure I would have chosen it. That would have been a huge mistake, because I would have deprived Derek of the most gifted teacher I have ever met.

Michele is presently nominated for teacher of the year in our state and has received several other accolades, many of which I have personally nominated her for as a way of expressing our appreciation. The following are two such letters I recently came across that will shed some light on the kind of teacher who impacts children in wonderful ways:

Michele Dickerson is my autistic son's special education teacher at Seth Woodard Elementary School. His self-contained classroom has the most severely affected children in our district. Dealing with such a wide range of disabilities, she and her staff face unbelievable daily challenges. They meet these challenges with skill, warmth, and energy. All of "her kids" adore her, and she is highly regarded by both peers and superiors.

Michele provides her students with opportunities most would not otherwise experience. She does whatever it takes to make sure each and every child can participate in all class activities. Michele sees no obstacles, only paths. Every week the entire class goes bowling, shopping, out to lunch, and swimming. At school, each student is assigned daily jobs, such as delivering mail, watering flowers, and serving food in the cafeteria. They are very proud to be helpful and productive, and they learn valuable vocational skills.

For years, Michele has volunteered as the district's coach for the Special Olympics. This involves after-school practices, trips to both district and state competitions, and an awards banquet. She even drives the busload of her champions across the state for the final competition. They get to stay in a hotel and eat out in restaurants, and huge fun is had by all.

Michele Dickerson is truly a gifted teacher who is determined to see that each of her students reaches his or her potential while enjoying the process. She richly deserves this honor.

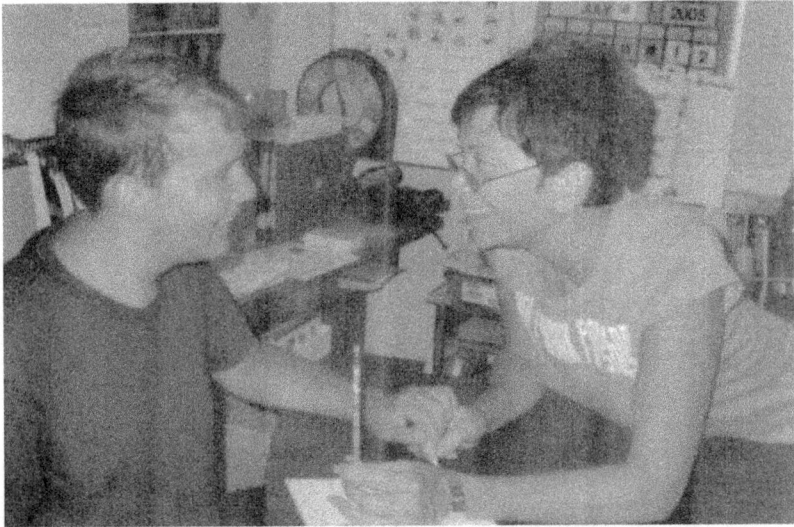

Derek and Michele

This letter is to nominate Michele Dickerson for teacher of the year. This honor would be a small token of appreciation for the peace of mind brought to us by the placement of our son in her class.

My [then] eight-year-old son is autistic and nonverbal and has quite a repertoire of idiosyncratic "behaviors." He poses many challenges, especially with regards to his education. Knowing that we would soon be leaving the nurturing environment of his early childhood center, which we had grown so accustomed to, my anxiety grew. When exploring the few options available, we faced panicked expressions and unanswered phone calls. No one wanted my son, Derek. Then we met Michele. The IEP [individual education plan] team consulted with her for ideas—and ideas we got. She was not only receptive to having Derek in her classroom, I later learned that she quietly campaigned for his placement.

However obvious, the realization that one's child doesn't belong in a "normal" classroom can be tough, but it is easily ameliorated by professionals who are competent, compassionate, and highly dedicated. Michele is one such professional. She not only is willing to "put up with" Derek, she is determined to teach him. Not being that familiar with autism at the time, she took it upon herself to be trained in the TEACCH [Treatment and Education of Autistic and related Communication-handicapped Children] curriculum and offered team conferences at her home during the summer to share her newly gained knowledge with the various therapists who would also be working with Derek. She also recently attended the ASW [Autism Society of Washington] annual conference and invited me to go with her. When she decided that her wealth of knowledge and experience might not adequately address some of Derek's unique needs, she sought out that information and successfully incorporated it into her classroom. We have already seen appreciable improvements in Derek's behavior at school. My son is only one of the very challenging children in Michele's classroom, and yet each of these children's unique needs is being superbly met.

When Derek dumps marbles out on the floor, throws toys out the window, tosses birdseed around the classroom, relieves himself in places other than those designated for such purposes, or screams uncontrollably for no apparent reason, Michele doesn't blink; she calmly and positively redirects him, patiently and persistently replacing unacceptable behaviors with those that are more appropriate and functional. Even when she is seriously cramping his style, Derek adores her.

We all feel very lucky to have this truly gifted teacher and tremendous human being in our lives. I would very much appreciate her being recognized for her many skills and qualities with this honor. She really is making a difference in the lives of "her kids" and their families.

Still Learning from Michele

I so admire Michele's persistence. As of this writing, she is teaching Derek, now eighteen, to read. After years of working with him, something finally clicked and he is making huge strides—a wonderful example of why one with a special-needs child should never give up. Michele and I are both so excited by the progress Derek has made this year; we don't want to do anything to derail it. He has had an explosion in his vocabulary, both of whole-language sight words and signs. At present he has in excess of 130 words and about 40 signs, all of which he has learned in the last year. I have always suspected that he had some sight words but couldn't figure out a way to verify it. When he was even about three or four, he could discriminate among five identical Sesame Street videos distinguishable only by their titles. He always picked the same favorite.

Michele's guidance over the years has been invaluable. She has taught me the importance of reintroducing material to Derek and using different tactics at different times, because no one can predict when something may gel with him. A perfect example of this is the aforementioned strides in Derek's reading and communication. He has always been a very reluctant reader and now is usually quite willing. The transformation is truly phenomenal.

Derek was Michele's first student with autism, and yet this lack of experience did not preclude her from being a most effective teacher. She actively sought out knowledge and suggestions from experts. We attended many conferences together over the years, gathering information to use with Derek. One important lesson she told me was not to make a student fit a program; rather, make the program fit the needs of the individual. She believes that it is vital to teach to the child's strengths and not to the diagnosis. We both agree that high, yet realistic expectations are a must for student's success. The ultimate goal should be for the student to become as independent as possible, with learned skills generalized into all aspects of his or her life—individuals with autism tend to compartmentalize newly learned skills to only the setting in which they are learned. For example, although Derek likes to read at school, he is very reluctant to do so at home. In his mind, reading is for school; Disney movies are for home.

The most basic advice Michele would like to impart is to be patient, persistent, and consistent. Eye contact is important to engage the student. This was a big issue when Derek first came to Michele's class, and now it is a nonissue. One-on-one teaching, with support as needed, is the best situation to teach skills and curriculum. Sitting across a table and facing the student, with the support person or helper standing behind the child, works well. We do this when Derek needs prompting and physical and verbal cues when he is attempting to write or learn new material. It is best to start out with hand-over-hand intervention, and then fade to wrist, then elbow, to verbal cue, and then, hopefully, no cues at all.

It is also important to find the most functional form of communication to use for each child. Michele has found various forms of discrete trial to be effective with all of her students. Discrete trial training (DTT) is a specific teaching method used to maximize learning for individuals with autism. For an in-depth explanation of this and other teaching and behavioral interventions, see two excellent Web sites: www.polyxo.com and www.autismtreatment.

info. Manipulation or the use of functional objects, imitation, reinforcers, and errorless learning are other strategies that Michele incorporates in her lessons—all of which have been successful with Derek. Schedules and routines are important for predictability. Michele uses prevocational work boxes and activity assignment strips to teach task completion and make it clear what is expected of the students and when they have successfully completed their assignment. After completing the assignment, Michele has the student select a reward from an array of appropriate choices. Derek's top three rewards now are coffee, pretzels, or swinging on the playground when the weather is nice.

Derek has made some great strides with his recent burst of learning, but I sometimes still measure Derek's life by the milestones we have or have not reached. At one point, we were told that if he could not read by age seven, he never would—and now, at age eighteen, he is reading. Every kid is unique, and that's no different for kids with autism. Derek's greatly increased vocabulary has also triggered more attempts at vocalization. He will make the sound for the beginning consonants of some words he is being asked to identify. For some familiar words, he is imitating the mouth movements to pronounce them. When he is given more ways to communicate, he is more likely to be understood, which greatly reduces his frustration and increases his attempts to communicate. This has very much been the case this year.

Twice, Derek has "commented" or labeled an observation—he had never done this before. The first time, I was coming through the door, carrying some sunflowers, and he signed "flowers." Most recently, our silly cat was tearing around the house, chasing something imaginary. Derek was giggling, and then looked at me and signed "funny cat." This may not sound like much, but it is a huge milestone for kids like Derek.

Previously, the only time Derek chose to communicate was to request something—usually something to eat. But, he would also use sign language to ask to go out or to the bathroom. I have always been very persistent with Derek, but I have had to learn more patience from Michele. Derek is very perceptive and responsive to dissention and negative tones of voice. He will sense my frustration when I think he isn't attending, and he will immediately shut down. So Michele has not only worked her magic with Derek, she has taught me many lessons as well. Until recently, I wasn't aware of how much Derek really does want to be successful and how eager he is to please. His academic sessions with Michele each morning are taxing for him, but the self-satisfaction and response to praise is obvious. When Michele and I tell him what a good job he is doing and how smart he is, he beams with pride. He doesn't enjoy the work, but he enjoys his success. I have always tried hard to guard against parental transference or misinterpretation to avoid deluding myself about Derek, so to finally see inherent satisfaction from him is priceless.

Chapter 7

HIGH SCHOOL BLUES

When it became increasingly obvious that Derek, now seventeen, was clearly the biggest kid in his elementary school and the only student who shaved, we knew his placement was no longer appropriate; his transition to high school was imminent. Students can sometimes stay in self-contained classrooms at their elementary schools until they are twenty-one, but they are typically medically or physically fragile. Usually at fourteen or fifteen, students transfer to middle school (grades six through eight). At age eighteen, those who are able enter into a transition or job-training program available through the high school. We charmed and weaseled our way around middle school altogether, but Derek's transfer to high school now became a reality. Because of the close relationships we all formed over the years, Michele and I would get misty-eyed whenever we talked about planning the transfer process. We also knew that Derek was going to struggle with such a huge change in environment and personnel. It was especially hard to make this transition because of how well he had been doing.

We decided that it would be best if he spent the last month of the school year at the high school so that he could become familiar with his new staff and surroundings. He would start with a half-day and increase his time as he could tolerate it. It sounded like a reasonable plan, but Derek wasn't having any of it. The novelty of his situation wore off after the first day. His teacher decided that he and Derek's aide, both big men, would meet me at the drop-off location and escort Derek into the classroom. They didn't even make it across the entranceway before Derek blew and bolted from his escorts. They then thought that I should bring him a bit later, when there was less commotion, after the bell rang and all of the students were in their classrooms. With this strategy, they made it as far as the cafeteria. Whenever there is an "incident" with a student involving any kind of violence or aggressive behavior, the district's policy is to write a report and put in the student's file. Derek racked up about nine incident reports during his first two weeks at the high school. It became so bad that I had to come and get him three times during that same period.

I decided to walk him to his classroom in the morning, as he seemed to have the most anxiety being escorted to class. This helped some, and he finished the final days of the school year without any major incidents.

That summer, Derek floated in the warm water of the swimming pool in peace with no one to "harsh his mellow." But fall approached way too soon for us all, and high school began in earnest. The first day went without a hitch or a tantrum. Derek's teacher and I remarked smugly on our success. Our pride, however, was short-lived. Day two was a disaster; we didn't even make it to the front door. As soon as I pulled into the school parking lot, Derek began making high-pitched whining noises that I know are a sign of anxiety. He got wild-eyed as the teachers came for him and strongly resisted as they tried to escort him into the building. I could hear him screaming the whole way. I sat in the car and waited for the cell phone to ring. Why waste the gas driving home when I knew I'd be called back? It took three minutes.

By the end of the first month, I was told that three different aides had quit because Derek was too difficult to handle. I was asked to keep Derek home on fourteen of the first thirty days of school because they didn't have adequate personnel to control him. After becoming increasingly frustrated with the situation and displeased with the person designated to be Derek's one-on-one aide, I decided to offer to just do it myself. It seemed silly and obvious at the same time. The school couldn't get this deal signed and sealed fast enough. I called them on Friday and began as Derek's mom/aide on Monday. Compared to the salary I would be making as a nurse if I were able to work while Derek was in school, the pay was insulting. However, the peace of mind was priceless.

I asked for one consideration: that Derek would still be able to meet with Michele every day to continue her reading program that had been so successful. After months of withdrawal, Derek's "vocabulary" grew and grew with each Michele fix. We went back to the elementary school every morning before school for an hour. We also went swimming at the YMCA and bowling every week with Michele's class. We also accompany them once a month to go grocery shopping and to the mall to eat lunch at the food court.

When Derek got anxious at high school, we walked around the track. I calculated that we did about seven hundred laps during the first school year. On especially stressful days, we walked as far as five miles. We had only one mild behavioral hiccup and zero incident reports. Eventually, we established a tenuous rapport with the high school staff. They slowly won Derek over with peace offerings of candy, gum, and the occasional donut. Derek still remained distrustful of most of the teachers because he didn't know what to expect from them or what they were going to expect of him. He made friends with one aide named Sandy, who he especially enjoyed sniffing because of her perfume and Derek's olfactory hypersensitivity, which can be associated with autism. I am sure he didn't remember that she was one of his aides at his preschool when he was three.

We were largely and happily ignored in our little corner where we worked on puzzles, worksheets, and vocational skills boxes. On really good days, we stopped at the store on the way home for a treat. I can't say that Derek enjoyed being at the high school, but he became accustomed to his new routine and tolerated it fairly well. In our state, special education students have to stay in high school until they are twenty-one to continue to receive benefits and services from state agencies and programs. Derek will also be getting job training at high school that will hopefully lead to some kind of employment at some point. It would be much easier for everyone to let Derek just stay home, but I think it is important to allow him social interaction and give him opportunities to continue to learn and grow.

As the end of spring approached that year, Derek became restless. He was already in summer mode, regardless of everyone else's timeline. When Derek came upstairs one morning, I could tell that his mood was fair to party cloudy with a chance of thunder. I can usually discern what kind of day it's going to be by Derek's initial facial expression. From the scowl on his face, I knew this day was going to be iffy, at best.

While I was in the laundry room trying to get the clothes folded before leaving for school, I could hear running water in the kitchen. When I went to check on him, I saw that Derek was gulping water. He had drunk so much that he began to vomit—everywhere. (At least, it was mostly water!) Of course, this occurred just after Derek took his medicine. Not being sure whether the medicine came up with the water, I erred on the side of caution and repeated his dose, remembering a past major tantrum on the elementary school playground that garnered a captive audience. We canceled our academic time with Michele while our moods and Derek's gastroenterology had time to settle and then headed to the high school—with some trepidation. As we pulled into the parking lot, Derek handed me a Coke bottle half full of urine. I guess some of that gulped water did make it through, enough that he couldn't wait to use the bathroom at school—a fifteen-minute drive from our home.

Derek seemed happy enough as we entered the building, probably anticipating a lunch of foods he usually doesn't get at home. However, just after lunch, he asked to use the restroom twice within a five-minute period—an escape technique and definite warning that he is becoming anxious. (When he is stressed at school, he will request to go to the bathroom just so he can hide from everyone in there.) He then cleared his desk and put his chair on top of it, communicating loud and clear that his school day was *over*. The problem was that we still had two hours of school left and had already left early three of the last five days.

Derek usually likes walking on the track as a release when he's tense, frustrated, or agitated but not on this day. I told him that we would go outside for a walk, but for some reason, he just wanted to be home. When we headed for the track and not the car, he let out high-pitched, piercing animal noises that would alarm anyone. I was able to lunge quickly enough to grab the coat he was wearing before he was able to bolt toward a group of students on the walkway. I tried to calm him down and walked him as quickly as possible to the car. Thankfully, most of the students and staff were in class. Those we did pass didn't seem to notice the glazed-over, wide-eyed look on this eager summer-breaker on early release. When there seems to be no reason for Derek's aberrant (even for him) behaviors, we wonder whether he just isn't feeling well and is frustrated that he can't communicate that to us.

I was welcomed home to a message on the answering machine from the school district office, saying that Derek's assessment and IEP were out of compliance with state regulations and that an "emergency meeting" was scheduled for the next morning. I had informed Derek's high school teacher of the IEP deficits six months earlier. That night, I think I had wine with/for dinner.

Chapter 8

AGGRESSION

The hardest thing for me to accept about Derek's autism is his angry aggression. It became especially problematic when he went through puberty and grew into a strong adult with the build of a fullback. His aggression became scary and dangerous. When he is not anxious, he is affable, funny, and at times, even charming. It is fairly easy to tell when he's becoming agitated. He gives several warning signs such as pacing, scowling, and whining that steadily escalate to jumping, screaming, and lunging.

When he transferred to Seth Woodard Elementary School, I stopped letting Derek ride the bus after he hit two of his fellow students. Some of the kids he is around are still small, and some are medically and physically fragile. It is mortifying to me to know that my child is capable of hurting someone else's. Historically, Derek has mainly gone after adults who are frustrating him by requesting tasks he would prefer not to do or causing him anxiety by putting him in unfamiliar situations that are in contrast to his daily routine. Some just happen to be in the wrong place at the wrong time when he happens to blow for no apparent reason. That it is not apparent does not mean that there was no precursor or antecedent; we just weren't paying enough attention to figure it out. Usually Derek is just trying to escape from an uncomfortable situation. Sometimes, being a rotten teenager and being a teenager with autism are not mutually exclusive.

At his elementary school, Derek punched a female aide so

hard that she had to wear a neck brace. At the high school he still attends, he came from behind and over his large desk and attacked the muscular track coach, ripping off his shirt. Last year, he even went after his aide, who was six foot eight. Both of these guys are athletic and had been professional football players. The latter quit because "it was too stressful being with Derek all day." I just smiled when the school officials told me this and wondered what they thought it was like for me. The high school then asked the wrestling coach to fill in as Derek's aide until they could find someone else to hire. Both of Derek's teachers are also men who were former athletes. The truth is that all of them are capable of containing Derek, but they don't feel comfortable with the degree of physical restraint required. I'm sure their main concerns are with possible liability and the district's policy of providing the least restrictive environment for the students. I think they were all relieved when I agreed to be with him at school.

Before I became Derek's aide, I would get a frantic phone call from the school when he became aggressive. I would race to the scene and find that Derek had expended all of his pent-up, angry energy. He would be as exhausted as the staff was trying to contain him. I have definitely seen major blowups but never witnessed a full-blown assault. I'm usually just there for the aftermath. I made the mistake of taking Derek home after such incidents, which rewarded his negative behavior and was unnecessary because we have never experienced more than one violent episode in a single day. I should have given him extra work to complete while expecting him to finish his school day.

When Derek was about twelve, his most serious assault was on his teacher Michele. To this day, no one can figure out what set him off; he was usually so excited when he realized that he was going swimming with his class. I was at home when the first phone call came. It was the school secretary, saying that I had to get to the YMCA right away because Derek was on a field trip there and had had a meltdown. I left immediately. I had just recently and reluctantly purchased a cell phone, as I am a bit of a Luddite, and the first call I received was from the school nurse who was on scene with Michele and her class. While on the way, I got at least three more calls from various school personnel telling me to get to the YMCA as quickly as possible. What I could gather from the frantic calls was that Derek became very agitated upon entering the building. Michele tried to contain him by forcing him into a dressing room and blocking the door from the inside. Derek attacked her when she prevented him from exiting.

As I entered the building, the nurse called yet again. I told her I had arrived and asked for their exact location. I could hear screaming in the background, and then I heard the screaming inside the Y. A small crowd of people were standing outside the dressing room door—some familiar, some not. Two were large male lifeguards. I wondered why everyone was just standing there while Michele was being attacked; it had taken me at least fifteen minutes to get there. Michele opened the door when she heard my voice. She was crying and visibly shaken. She had many bloody scratches, bite marks, and bruises. Derek's eyes were glazed over like someone who had had a seizure. His chest heaved. When I shouted his name, he recognized my voice. His eyes cleared, and he quickly regained composure. It took Michele and me a little longer.

We cried, hugged, and tended wounds. I glared at the gawking group as we passed through them. When we walked out, Derek gently took Michele's arm to escort her, as he so often does. I'm positive that he didn't even know what had just happened. On that day, I knew for sure that going back to work simply wasn't an option, as I would be accompanying Derek to school so such an awful scene could not replay itself.

Everyone comments that Derek behaves only for me, even though he outweighs me by nearly one hundred pounds and is almost a foot taller. I think there is a kind of alpha-mom thing at work between us. From the time he was little, I never tolerated any aggressive behaviors. The only time Derek hurt me was accidental. When he was about thirteen, I was using the computer in the basement and heard Derek's agitated screaming. He was escalating fast. I ran up the stairs and almost made it to the top, when Derek bolted through the basement door on his way to his room. He spun me around as he quickly descended the stairs. I tried to get my balance, but I came down on my bad knee, which buckled immediately. I tumbled all the way down the staircase. I felt blood running down my neck even before I came to rest on the basement floor. My two front teeth were broken. The first pain I felt was in my knee, which was quickly swelling to the size of a cantaloupe. When I tried to move, pain shot through my shoulders and down my arms and back. I would later learn that two discs in my neck and two in my lower back were herniated. My shoulder was also injured, which made hobbling around on crutches for about two months even more difficult. My injuries are mostly healed now, but I still have occasional pain. Once you reach your forties, you just don't bounce back as well anymore; it takes a lot longer to heal.

I believe it was this incident and/or the trip to Mexico that caused me to reconsider putting Derek on medication. I had seen too many parents in the past who had used medications as a substitute for proper parenting to manage their kids and make them compliant. I didn't want to become one of those parents, so I had resisted medicating Derek a lot longer than I probably should have. I was also put off by the pages of side effects and adverse reactions that accompanied the medications—some of which are quite serious and permanent, though rare.

My husband spent an entire day researching and comparing all of the recommended medications. We consulted with Derek's pediatrician before deciding on a regimen to try. Within days of medicating Derek, everyone he was in contact with reported a noticeable improvement. The result was impressive. I really don't think I can control him anymore without medications and don't even want to think what our lives would be like without that help. (Readers can find descriptions of medications for treating behaviors associated with autism in chapter 22.)

A Terrible Misunderstanding

The following account is a tragic example of why I no longer let Derek out in public without Rex or me. I know there is a chance that something could set him off and cause him to act out aggressively. He would be misunderstood by those unfamiliar with him, and if someone called the police, he would not comply with their commands because he wouldn't understand them. Now that Derek is older and bigger, he would try to get away and probably fight back. He could very well end up in the exact same situation that I am about to describe. I introduce him to every officer we come in contact with and have sent his picture to the local police stations. I also plan to ask for permission to introduce him at roll call so as many officers as possible will know him. As careful as I am, Derek has already had one such unfortunate experience born of misunderstanding that involved the police. That was plenty.

I am still haunted by this recent tragedy that occurred in our community. A well-liked young man with a mental disorder had been living successfully on his own, working as a janitor through a community skills center. When he fell through the cracks, however, and stopped receiving adequate supervision, he stopped taking his medication, and his condition rapidly deteriorated. He stopped showing up for work and was acting bizarre in public. He approached a car with two young women in it. They were at an ATM withdrawing some money. When they saw him, they became afraid and pulled away before their transaction was complete. When they were what they thought was a safe distance, the women called 911 to report what they thought was an attempted robbery. They believed the man had taken their money and ATM card. He had not. The dispatcher who put out the report told the officer who answered the call that money had indeed been stolen and conveyed the description of the suspect and the location.

The patrol officer spotted the man entering a minimart and called for backup. He entered the store and approached the suspect with his nightstick already out. (All of this was being recorded on video.) The officer ordered him repeatedly to get down. He didn't. The officer told him to drop the bottle of pop he was holding; he didn't. When the officer hit him, the man resisted and tried to run away. By this time a second officer was on the scene. They both continued to hit and restrain the suspect, who was still actively resisting. They used a taser on him three times. More police came, and they finally controlled him with handcuffs and leg restraints. They positioned him face down and placed an oxygen mask over his face to prevent him from spitting. (No one reported, however, that he had been spitting.) No oxygen was connected to the mask, and there were no paramedics checking on him. Within minutes, the man turned blue and stopped breathing. Paramedics then came and transported him to the hospital, where he died about three days later.

I believe that a series of misunderstandings, miscommunication, lack of knowledge, overreaction, and largely an uncaring society caused the death of this innocent man. However, the official cause of death was determined to be asphyxiation and excited delirium.

Crisis Response for Derek Porter
WVHS/SPED
2007

Behaviors That Represent a Negative Escalation Cycle
- scowling
- restlessness
- compulsive tapping
- high-pitched whining

Possible Causes Precipitating an Escalation
- obsessing on desired food items (keep out of sight)
- negative behaviors in other students
- noise or commotion
- general overwhelming sensory input
- opportunity (lack of supervision)
- avoiding undesired tasks or demands

Prevention Strategy
- Change arrival time to avoid AM activity in halls—late arrival option.
- Give prn medication intervention at signs of agitation.
- Take Derek to outside track for a brisk walk.
- Keep coffee, pop, and any other desired food items out of sight.
- Have a backup person (besides Derek's aide) available at all times and check to see that walkie-talkies are in working order and on the same channel every morning.

- Ensure that communication system is in place—update cell phone numbers.

- Have staff completely trained on assertiveness and intervention.
- Practice emergency drill annually.
- Communicate/report any behavior problem promptly.

Crisis Response with Increased Escalation

- Aide will attempt to de-escalate with calm reassurance.
- Administer prn Risperdol dose (.5mg) as first signs of agitation.
- Attempt least restrictive response with Derek—assertive intervention.
- Have backup personnel (usually Mr. Cerenzia or Sandy) move other students away ASAP.
- Try to contain Derek in an area where he can de-escalate.
- Use evasive rather than restrictive action.
- Instruct Derek to "SIT DOWN!" verbally and by signing (this prevents him from being able to lunge).
- Engage communication system for overhead-page security response if necessary.

Chapter 9

WAAS/ABLLS

Washington Alternate Achievement System / Assessment of Basic Language and Learning Skills

In our state of Washington, students are required to pass a test in the tenth grade called the Washington Achievement System. Students with IEPs (individual education plans) who are not able to pass this test can instead have their teacher submit a portfolio of samples of their schoolwork. In 2005, Derek's teacher submitted his portfolio. It was beautifully done, but at that time Derek demonstrated no ability to read and only knew about ten signs. He was not able to draw or write and had no comprehension of numbers or money. The only samples of work representing his academic abilities or lack thereof would have been some scribbling with a marker or less-than-near approximations of tracing.

I was dismayed when I received an official letter from the governor and the superintendent congratulating Derek for meeting the states achievement standard in reading, writing, mathematics, and science, no less. *Really?* I sure would like to see the short list of just what those standards are. It stated that he demonstrated skills that would provide him access to opportunities in his future. He was commended for his hard work and focus and was encouraged to continue to set high goals. They must not have seen the same portfolio I did. Derek's teacher explained that the portfolios are really meant to hold the teachers accountable for the education of their special-needs students. I believe that these meaningless "feel good" form letters are to pacify parents with special-needs students.

It is understandably extremely difficult to test or assess nonverbal individuals with autism. Even when one suspects, as one should, that the child might have something intellectual going on, it is so hard for the child to demonstrate it on our terms. If it were possible to give Derek an IQ test, his score would be abysmally low. There are more appropriate tests for those with autism, but they are far from perfect. Derek has been assessed using the Assessment of Basic Language and Learning Skills (ABLLS), which consists of an assessment, a curriculum guide, and a skills-tracking system for children with autism or other developmental disabilities who have language delays. It also contains a task analysis of the many skills necessary to communicate. I was impressed with how much improvement Derek demonstrated compared to his assessment three years ago. I now think it so important to use the same test and the same examiner—who really knows the student—to achieve a meaningful comparison showing encouraging growth. This summary of Derek's assessment (written by Katrina, high school psychologist) lists all of the areas that are addressed:

Previous assessment with the ABBLS allowed for comparison of skill levels and provided the ability to identify the areas in which Derek had increased his skills:

2007 Assessment of Basic Language and Learning Skills Results

A. Cooperation and reinforcer effectiveness: Derek will readily take a reinforcer when offered and prefers edible to nonedible reinforcers. He also has begun to seek approval for task completion.

B. Visual performance: Derek has made improvements on many tasks in this area from the previous assessment. He has improved his ability to match identical pictures to objects, replicate block designs on a picture card, and put pieces in a form box/shape sorter. Derek has significantly improved his ability to complete puzzles (score has increased from zero to the maximum of four in most areas of puzzle completion). Derek has also demonstrated that he is better able to identify a previously presented item from a group, arrange picture cars in sequence, and draw lines from start to finish in a simple maze (this was a task he was not able to do three years ago).

C. Receptive language: Derek has increased the number of objects and pictures of items he is able to identify (to fifty or more) from a selection of two. He has increased his skill in selecting specified pictures or objects from a larger selection of three or more. His ability to select two specified objects from a larger selection of objects has increased from not able to perform three years ago, to a maximum score on this task. Derek is also now better able to follow an instruction such as "Give Jim a hug." He is better able to use motor skills in response to requests to touch, point to, get the, or give me. Derek is also now able to learn to select a picture of an object after being required to select the item within five presentations, a skill he did not demonstrate at the last reevaluation. Derek can identify at least four items/ sounds that correspond to each other, a task he was not previously able to perform. He has also developed the ability to select two items in a specified sequence (e.g., Touch the shoe, then touch the sock). Derek is also able to select items that are the same (but still struggles with the concept of different) from an array of items. Derek has begun to select the item that is a nonexample from an array of items (e.g., not food). He is also better at selecting pictures of scenes or activities if it is a specific learned activity. His ability to select pictures representing emotions is much improved from at least one emotion to at least four emotions.

D. Imitation: Derek continues to have strength in the area of imitation. He still does not spontaneously imitate or show the ability to demonstrate after a delay, but he has developed the ability to imitate motor movements such as facial and head movements that are being done by others. He can imitate up to ten sequences of two actions (e.g., he is asked to do this: and the teacher will clap hands then tap thighs, and he will imitate.

E. Vocal imitation: Derek is primarily nonverbal, but he has learned to imitate sounds on request and imitates some initial sounds of words (e.g., for shoe say *sh*).

F. Requests: This is Derek's primary form of interaction. He will ask for (by gesture or sign) an increased number of items/activities when the reinforcer is present and a word or sign is given (pretzels, crackers, candy, apple, bathroom, outside, cookie, bread, popcorn, out, peanut). He scored the maximum points possible on his ability to request with the preferred item present when asked "What do you want?" using either words or signs. Derek uses signs to request future items or events and has made the most progress in this area by developing the ability to spontaneously request (by signing) objects, action, or information throughout the day. He will sign or gesture for coffee, cracker, gum, and more. He signs "pretzel" and gives a bowl. He signs "coffee" and gives a cup.

G. Labeling: Derek is limited to signs, which he uses to request/label, and has learned to label more things such as body parts (which he points to). He knows when there is an obvious problem, such as when someone he knows well is hurt or needs help. His ability to label common environmental sounds has improved from none to at least eight. This means that when Derek hears a sound, he will point to the picture that goes with that sounds. This is a new ability.

H. Intraverbals: Derek is nonverbal, with vocalizations, and uses limited signs, but he has increased the number of words he can sign: peanuts, popcorn, cracker, coffee, candy, cocoa, pretzel, French fries, finished, thank-you, more, in, out , bathroom, apple, please, and pop.

I. Spontaneous vocalizations: Derek shows more spontaneous vocalizations than when previously assessed. His vocalizations are approximations of words said by others. He spontaneously requests items or actions (by signing) at least ten times per day and has begun to use spontaneous verbal approximations (for popcorn).

J.   Syntax and grammar: Derek is nonverbal.

K.   Play and leisure: Derek has good ability to enjoy play
     and activities. He enjoys many physical activities
     (walking, swinging, and swimming), will observe others,
     and prefers solo activities. He has very limited ability
     with computers. His repertoire of activities has increased
     to include 25+ piece puzzles, simple dot-to-dots, and
     putting tokens into a slotted box. Derek can engage in
     any of these activities for at least fifteen minutes, which
     is an increase in the length of his attention to a task.

L.   Social interaction: Derek's ability to interact socially
     has grown to include waving and approximating the
     word *bye* verbally. He also shows more curiosity in the
     behavior of his peers. Much of his social interaction
     will happen with siblings and people he knows well.
     He has developed more ability to ask (sign) for items
     from peers. Although he doesn't spontaneously label
     items for others, he will label by signing or pointing, on
     request. In regard to sharing items, Derek will become
     passive when another wants what he has but will
     reluctantly share a pretzel to an extended hand. Derek
     continues to have a behavior management plan to assist
     in controlling and monitoring behavior outbursts in
     school, but this has been rarely used this school year.
     (Derek's mother has accompanied him throughout the
     day for most of the school year. He responds well to his
     mother and her presence decreases his agitation.)

M.   Group instruction: Derek has grown to incorporate
     the ability to sit appropriately in large groups, a skill he
     was reluctant to perform three years prior. He would
     still prefer to avoid these situations. He also shows

improvement in attending to his teacher and other student's responses during small-group instruction. Derek is able to get up from a group and walk around when he has had enough. If prompted, Derek can follow instructions presented to a group. Derek does his best in a 1:1 instructional setting using discrete trial format to learn a skill.

N. Classroom routine: This is an area of strength for Derek. Derek is now able to line up in the lunch line upon request. He has learned to get and return his own educational materials independently. His ability to work independently on academic activities has increased to ten minutes, and he physically transitions to the next area or activity with prompting. Derek has good ability to wait in line for lunch and to take a turn in a learned activity.

O. Generalized responding: Derek has already shown the ability to generalize across stimuli (e.g., if a cup is brown or green, it is still a cup). Now he is also able to show generalization of responding to something he sees or to questions. He has also acquired the ability to receptively identify the function of something and, conversely, identify something by its function. He does this using gestures and signs.

P. Reading skills: Derek's reading ability is an area of great improvement. He reads primarily by demonstrating understanding of words he has learned by sight or sound, although he does vocalize some approximations of words and letter sounds. He twice identified B from a field of three, matches words to the same word in a different font, and approximates reading *ball* and *boy* by pointing to and naming the letters.

Q. He does not decode words but indicates knowledge of whole known words. Derek reads about 120 sight words by pointing to the requested word. He can read simple three-to-six- word sentences, combining known words receptively by pointing. He is able to read: "sit in the chair" and then, sit in the chair, indicating reading comprehension.

R. Math skills: Derek's math skills remain constant. He is nonverbal and cannot sign numbers, so this limits his ability to demonstrate understanding and naming of numbers. Given a field of two numbers or asked to identify a requested amount, Derek is inconsistent with his responses. He does not understand the value of coins but knows that when he gives dollars to the lady at Wendy's, she gives him food. He has learned that if he points to the number three, he will get more candy than if he points to one. This is his limited understanding of 1:1 correspondence.

S. Writing: Derek has improved to be able to color between lines. He is now able to trace straight and curved lines and neatly copy curved lines and shapes (matching size, shape, and orientation). This is an area of great improvement for Derek. He can trace some letters independently but has little tolerance for it.

T. Spelling: Derek can match letters for words up to three letters when not given extra letters. With prompts, he matches individual letters to letters on cards for words up to three letters in length when not given extra letters.

U. Dressing skills: Derek's dressing skills have improved in areas of putting his socks on and off, using snaps and buttons, and adjusting his clothing when needed. He still struggles with using unattached zippers and tying shoes. He can dress independently but will often have his clothes inside out or backwards.

V. Eating skills: Derek is independent in is eating skills and has developed the ability to use a knife to spread peanut butter on bread. He has been able to pour liquid into a cup since the age of three.

W. Grooming: Most of Derek's grooming requires verbal or gestural prompts (i.e., wash hands, brush teeth). He has become independently able to brush his teeth but still has to be monitored. He is able to brush his hair with prompting.

X. Toileting skills: Derek's can perform toileting skills independently except for wiping himself after a bowel movement.

Y. Gross motor skills: Derek can perform all gross motor skills listed in the assessment. He has now learned to kick a ball at a target, ride a three-wheel scooter, do jumping jacks, climb a ladder, and walk on a balance beam.

Z. Fine motor skills: Derek can now accurately place blocks on block design cards, snip paper with scissors, and color within boundaries. He is now able to perform all skills listed in the assessment, except for copying shapes and patterns.

This assessment not only shows areas in which Derek has grown in the last three years, it also shows deficits in areas that we can continue to work on. This assessment is an excellent source for making future IEP goals, as it clearly shows areas we need to work on.

Derek's teacher and school psychologist decided that the ABLLS assessment was the most appropriate for him and I agreed; however, other assessments may be better suited for other children with different needs or deficits. Over seventy different assessments are available from an online site, www.superduperinc.com. I recommend discussing with the child's teacher, therapists, and psychologist which assessments would be most appropriate and useful. The following are some with which I am familiar:

- Dr. Eric Schopler, founder of the TEACCH program, has developed an excellent assessment for children with autism called CARS (Childhood Autism Rating Scale). It contains fifteen scales that an evaluator scores, following a diagnostic session determining the severity of autistic behavior.

- The BRIAAC, or Behavior Rating Instrument for Autistic and Atypical Children (Kalish, Ruttenberg, Werner, and Wolf), provides eight scales measuring the child's relationship with adults, communication vocalization and expressive speech, sound and speech reception, social responsiveness, body movement, and psychobiological development.

- The Behavior Observation System, or BOS (Freemen, Ritvo, Guthrie, Schroth, and Ball), is made up of nine three-minute observations that record the presence of behaviors associated with autism. The BRIACC, CARS, and BOS describe behavior of the child and are considered primarily diagnostic; they aren't that helpful in establishing IEP goals. The Autism Screening Instrument for Educational Planning, ASIEP (Krug,

Arick, and Almond), better serves this function. It contains a behavior checklist, instructions on obtaining samples of vocalizations, an interaction assessment, an educational assessment, and a prognosis of learning rate. It can provide useful information about the educability of the child. It addresses the learning environment as well as academic skills.

- Another ecobehavioral evaluation is the Code for Instructional Structure and Student and Academic Response (Greenwood and Stanley). This has allowed for the identification of useful instructional interactions that best suit the individual student.

- The revised PEP, or Psychoeducational Profile (Schopler and Reichler), focuses on the child's development in the areas of imitation, perception, fine motor skills, gross motor skills, and cognitive verbal skills.

- The Personal Futures Planning, or PFT (Mount and Zwernick), is a profile cooperatively developed by those with ongoing relationships with the child. A team consisting of parents, educators, and therapists set goals that can be used in the IEP. The student's preferences are discussed to determine what will best motivate the student to learn.

- There is also the Checklist for Autism in Toddlers (CHAT) screening tool, which should be used by the pediatrician for every child at his or her eighteen-month well-baby checkup. A copy of it, along with an excellent video titled The Importance of Early Autism Diagnosis, can be obtained from Families for Early Autism Treatment (FEAT). Their Web site is www.feat.org. In Washington, it is www.featwa.org.

Chapter 10

IEP: INDIVIDUAL EDUCATION PLAN

When a child with a disability enters the public school system, an individual education plan (IEP) is implemented. The child's IEP is meant to address the specific needs of the student to best facilitate his or her learning. Key elements of a successful IEP include goals of the IEP that are meaningful, measurable, and obtainable or realistic. When these are truly the goals and there is a reasonably responsive school district, the result will be a useful IEP that will benefit the child. If the IEP process becomes contentious, it is the child who ultimately loses out. While the tug-of-war continues between school and parents, very little is being done to help the child. These battles can drag out for years, resulting in costly legal bills and a less-than-ideal result. When the situation becomes an ugly battle between district budget constraints and unrealistic parents, no one wins. Demanding unfounded and expensive therapies is not a good way to start out.

I have always tried to be fair but vigilant. I have been very fortunate in most of my experiences with my school district. We have had a cooperative relationship since Derek began preschool at the age of three, and I have always been a strong advocate for my son. None of us were perfect, but all of us tried to do what was best for Derek. I know that horror stories about unresponsive districts with clueless or abusive staff abound, but I really don't think this is the norm. If you have a child with autism and your school district is one of those, either move or be prepared to go to the mat. The laws are on your side.

As we—Derek's preschool teachers and therapists and I—were all new at this "autism thing," we worked as a team trying to figure out what worked and what didn't. We followed models and techniques from established, successful programs (such as TEACCH). We attended conferences and in-services to learn as much as we could, and I believe that we got it mostly right. If anyone tells you they have "the" formula that will cure your child, run away. If they tell you that they have behavioral strategies involving discrete trial and successful learning, you're probably in the right school. Don't trust theories—make sure the practices decided upon are consistently carried out.

I've gotten spoiled over the past eleven years because Derek's teacher, Michele, not only writes excellent IEPs, she also implements them with fervor. It wasn't until we were finally drop-kicked to the high school that I even had to think about Derek's IEP again. When he was little, I would write a list of goals and give it to the preschool. The school officials would include them on their forms, and we would all sign it and work toward meeting those goals during the school year. Sometimes we were successful, sometimes not, although I usually thought we were making progress, even when it was at a maddeningly slow pace. Michele's IEPs for Derek usually exceeded my high expectations, and I eventually declined meetings and would sign them sight unseen. We always seemed to be on the same page in terms of goals for Derek, and we have always worked together as a team. She is so respected in our district that when she requests something for her kids, such as special curriculum or software, it is usually forthcoming.

Derek's last IEP was written by a teacher who only had him

for about three months before his IEP became due. The teacher didn't really even know him, his strengths, or his deficits. In addition, the district implemented new, unfamiliar software that had limited selections in various categories from which to choose. We went from having a really great IEP to one that was not even functional. It was a meaningless form with random checklists and inappropriate formulated goals. It had no transition plan and did not address any of Derek's many challenges or needs. It was flagged and sent back by the state because it was out of compliance with state law. It took the state's rescinding Derek's funding to finally get the attention of the district. At the end of last year, the director of special education scrambled to submit a transition plan that should have been done by the teacher.

As it stands now, I will be at school with Derek assuring that his needs are met, so the IEP is a formality at this point. But, because of the disappointing way his IEP was handled last year, I will be requesting a planning meeting with formal representation from state and local advocacy groups. I feel protective of the other special-needs kids in our district and want the schools to know that they have a responsibility to get it right. IEPs are not just a nuisance for teachers; they are indeed a plan to follow to ensure that each child is getting an appropriate and valuable education. It is important to know one's rights and to be familiar with the laws in your state. A very helpful Web site in this regard is www. wrightslaw.com.

Until one is familiar and comfortable with the IEP process, he or she should be accompanied by someone who is. Cooperation and support from the school staff should be expected rather than a situation that is adversarial. I have found that most special-education teachers want their students to be successful and understand that a team approach in developing the IEP will produce the best outcome. A good IEP that everyone is happy with is a tool that makes each person's life easier, or in the case of the child, at least better. IEPs are designed to challenge the child so that growth can occur, but the goals should not be so lofty that they cause the child daily frustration that translates into negative behaviors. This would definitely be defeating the purpose.

Prepare for the planning meeting by making a list of goals. If a spark of interest in the child is noticed, it should be written down. It could be the basis of a new learning strategy. Follow the lead of the child; it is much easier to teach a child with what he or she is interested in. Many autistic children have such limited interests that it is difficult to come up with novel ways to keep them attending for successful learning.

It is important to be clear and direct when informing those at the meeting what the expectations are. Be forthcoming with any unpleasant behaviors that your child has. That which is not addressed, can't be helped. There is absolutely no shame in admitting that you need help. It took me years to admit this even to myself. I am independent to a fault, which probably denied Derek access to help that was available to him at various times in our lives. When the IEP is written and presented, the parents or their advocate needs to check it to see whether each goal is meaningful, measurable, and realistic; those that are not should be challenged. A plan that is insufficient in any way should not be signed or accepted.

Parents should prepare for the planning meeting by making a list of goals they have for their child. Here are some of the goals for Derek that I have come up with for next year:

- Expand the use of sight words to include requests, labeling, and sentence construction.

- Increase sign language usage, both receptive and expressive.
- Support further 1:1 correspondence learning.
- Reinforce color identification verbally and with matching.
- Encourage commenting and labeling in his environment by rewarding any attempt with praise and repeated response.
- Encourage new interest in computer game by offering it as a "break" from work
- Decrease outbursts by reducing anxiety and agitation, offering gross motor activities such as swinging, walking, or jumping before escalation. Administer prn medications when appropriate.
- Have him learn and use new schedules for fall routine.
- Help him learn his new school menu so that he can order independently.
- Increase independence with activities of daily living.
- Find appropriate jobs that he can do at the school, such as sorting recyclables, shredding papers, watering plants, and picking up trash.

I will have to quantify each of these goals so that they are measurable. (For example, state which percentage of the decided number of trials will be expected: Derek will identify 150 sight words from an array of four with 90 percent accuracy.) Data collection is a tedious, yet necessary and important element of the IEP process. One can't know whether the IEP was successful without data to measure progress or lack thereof.

Parents know their children better than anyone, so they should make sure the number of requests is realistic and meaningful and not overwhelming for the child. It is sometimes a precarious balance to state goals that are challenging without their being overly frustrating.

Remember that an IEP is just a plan—hopefully, a good one—but it is not cast in stone. It is a work in progress to be changed or adjusted by the teacher or appropriate specialist, as necessary, to keep it functional. Parents should request a meeting any time they believe a change is needed.

Chapter 11

WANDERLUST

From the time Derek could walk, he was quite the little escape artist. Over the years we tried every gadget and gizmo known to humankind to try to contain him. We had a motion-detecting laser alarm that shot across the driveway. It worked okay, but the critters (deer, porcupines, raccoons, coyotes) would set it off at all hours. Every time the alarm sounded, I would have to do the fifty-yard-dash to see whether the interloping creature was human or not. It lost any effectiveness it had when Derek eventually figured out that if he walked around the sensor beam, Mom didn't come chasing after him when he was trying to escape his compound.

We also tried an expensive harness-honing device that zipped up the back and looked impossible to get out of. We put it on Derek and let him outside. We followed the signal about fifty yards into the woods, thinking we were tracking Derek, but found that he had taken it off and tossed it into a bush. We found him clear on the opposite side of our ten-acre property.

I asked my vet if he would consider putting an identification chip in Derek, but he mumbled something about the FDA and declined. We have better ways of tracking our poodles than our children. We have sleigh bells on all of our doors so that we can hear when a door is being opened. Most people have doors that lock from the inside—not ours. We eventually put key locks on both the outside and the inside, so it usually takes about ten minutes to find the hidden key to unlock the door for the UPS delivery man.

We have to continually change the hiding places as Derek discovers them; this is not only a nuisance, it is also a fire hazard. The sliding doors are bolted shut, and all of the windows have locks.

When Derek was younger, none of these precautions were adequate when my little Houdini was on a mission. He once climbed out of his brother's second-story window and onto the garage roof. I'm still not sure how he got down and am probably better off not knowing. Sometimes he was on a mission towards a specific goal, and sometimes he just seemed to want to walk. When my parents were still living, we used to visit Florida annually. Derek would walk for miles on the beach with no particular destination in mind, as the direction he walked didn't seem to matter to him.

The following are some of the more memorable anecdotes of Derek's wandering adventures.

Derek Goes Long

I believe that even the best dads just do not have the same radar mommies do. Mothers predict rather than react. We know what sharp, hot, or breakable thing our little ones are going to reach for before they do. It is simply biological. It's not that I don't trust Rex; it's just that I'm somewhat overprotective.

When Derek was about two, I left him home with Rex, with some trepidation, while Whitney and I went to the store. Rex and a friend were watching a football game while Derek played on the floor. We got groceries and ran a couple of errands. When we returned after about ninety minutes, Rex and his friend were in the exact position we had left them in. I quickly scanned the room. "Rex, where's Derek?" As the words registered, Rex's eyes widened. "*Derek?*"

We did the "Porter scramble." I sent Whitney upstairs, Rex downstairs, and Rex's friend to the backyard. I knew we didn't pass Derek coming home, but he could be anywhere in that amount of time. We determined that the house was "clear" and started searching the woods of our ten-acre property. We called Derek's name in vain, knowing he wouldn't or couldn't answer. I don't remember how long we looked; but just as I was really starting to get worried, I saw what looked like a flag in a bush in the distance. As I got closer, I could make out the white turtleneck Derek had been wearing. I ran to the large syringa bush to find Derek hanging upside down, entangled by the branches. He must have fallen as he toddled and rolled downhill. He wasn't crying; he seemed more bewildered than anything.

Pantry Pest

One summer afternoon when Derek was about four, I answered the phone to hear an unfamiliar voice ask whether I had a little blond boy. She said that the boy had showed up at her home, and her neighbor believed he was a Porter. I told the woman that she must be mistaken because I had just put my son in the bathtub upstairs. No sooner had the words left my mouth than I looked toward the foyer and saw small, wet footprints leading to the open front door.

"Oh, my God! I'll be right there."

I got in the car and wound down our driveway. The house that Derek had wandered to was about a mile away. A pleasant woman met me at the front door and led me to her kitchen. There was Derek—buck naked—standing in the pantry and munching on Ritz crackers. He gave me that "Oh, hi, Mom" look. I thanked the woman, apologized, and explained my way to the front door with my little plundering explorer in tow.

My newly acquainted neighbor, though understanding, told me that she had seen a cougar in her yard only two days ago and that I really should be more careful. It's not likely I'll be nominated "Mother of the Year" by our homeowners association.

Preschooler MIA

The preschool secretary called, and speaking in a measured tone, told me that Derek, who was then three, was missing, but not to worry because the sheriff's department was combing the neighborhood for him. When I got to the school, everyone was scurrying all over the place. I decided to pretend that I was Derek, so I began in his classroom. It was probably time for the dreaded "circle time," and Derek decided to duck and run. At different times during the school day, Derek's teacher would ask the children to gather at the front of the room and sit on a large, oval rug. During the morning circle time, the group identified the day, month, and year and determined the weather. Other times, the circle (which was really an oval) was used for discussions, lessons, or stories. Nothing in circle time had any relevance for Derek, and an aide would have to hold him to get him to comply at all. Most circle times usually lasted about fifteen minutes, but the teacher set a timer for three minutes as the goal for Derek's endurance. Derek would rather spend the time playing in the sink or the sandbox and didn't understand why he wasn't allowed to do so.

Derek wasn't much of a hider; his usual M.O. was to put as much distance as possible between himself and his captors. We searched the building again while the sheriffs continued to scour the neighborhood. After about an hour, the janitor emerged holding Derek by the hand. He had found him in the janitorial closet playing with the tools in the toolbox. Derek was still holding a shiny red-and-silver screwdriver.

Derek also went missing at a field trip to Walk in the Wild Zoo, which covered about thirty acres. For over an hour, people were searching in all directions through the densely wooded park. They finally found Derek in the bathroom, happily playing with the water in the sink. We bought a harness and leash for the school. They had previously politely declined, citing "least restrictive environment" or something to that effect. "We don't treat our young charges like pets." That was the policy B.D. ... before Derek.

Neighbors

I was just home from the hospital after giving birth to Dylan. Derek was three at the time and had no sympathy for his funny-walking mommy; he did not curtail his wanderlust one bit. My being preoccupied with a newborn gave Derek new chances to escape for outdoor exploration, and when the first opportunity presented itself, he was gone. It is truly amazing the distance that Derek could cover in a matter of moments. I saw the front door ajar and waddled outside; no Derek. I made it down our 1,100-foot driveway; still no sign of him. On the lot next to ours, a new house was being built. Spotting workers atop the newly framed structure, I yelled to ask whether they could see a little blond boy. One of the workers spotted Derek and offered to "fetch him" for me. He was about a mile away and probably on his way to the house with the Ritz crackers. After a few minutes, the roofer rounded the switchback by our driveway. He had an unhappy Derek in a wheelbarrow and pushed him all of the way home for me. I believe this was when we put double locks on all the doors.

When the above-mentioned house was complete, a nice couple with a little boy about Derek's age (five) moved in. Their house was usually Derek's first stop whenever he escaped his domestic prison. The family gave him cookies and crackers when he "visited" and would loan him a T-shirt if he showed up *au naturel*. Once he walked into the house, down the hall, and right into Mrs. Stephen's bubble bath while she was still in it. The Stephens were able to laugh about this escapade, but Derek definitely nearly wore out his welcome on his next visit. Mr. Stephens had just finished installing a pump to the beautiful waterfall he had dug out and built by hand. Derek poured a giant bag of kitty litter into the flowing water. After I got the phone call, I grabbed my checkbook and hurried to pick up Derek. The burned-out pump motor was still smoking when I got there.

Usually his escape routes were fairly predictable, but every now and then he'd throw us a curve ball. I would sense that Derek was gone before I actually knew it. When he got a little older, he was so fast that I would have to use the car to catch him. One day when he ran off, I couldn't find him. I followed his usual path, questioning all the neighbors on the way. I went back home and called everyone who lived on our hill. No one had seen him. I prayed that this wasn't going to be the day when Derek decided to venture into the woods rather than just following the paved road. If he didn't take his usual route through our housing development, I would have no idea where to begin searching. We live right next to a nature reserve comprising about four hundred acres of woodland. It would take a large search party hours to cover that large an area, and we wouldn't even know if that was, in fact, where he was. I panicked when I thought of him alone in the woods at night. I had Rex overhead paged, and he hurried home to help me search.

I was just about to call the police when Whitney came walking down the driveway with Derek. She had ridden her bicycle up the cul-de-sac above us and found Derek throwing rocks in a puddle. He had never headed up the hill until then. His predictability had become unpredictable, and the scope of our searches had enlarged.

Derek does seem to go through stages with many of his behaviors, where suddenly an obsession will disappear and maybe resume years later or be replaced altogether with a totally different obsession. His escaping and wandering is a perfect example of this. As Derek has aged, he seems to have lost his desire to roam. The last time he escaped was about six years ago when he visited our new neighbors with my pruning shears and ended up in the back of a patrol car. I doubt it was that experience that curbed his compulsion to explore; it could be the medications that have helped, but it is so hard to guess what goes through his mind. I would give anything to be Derek for a day so that I could understand him better.

Chapter 12

HAPPY TRAVELER

Derek began his travels early in life. In his first year alone, he accumulated more frequent flyer miles than most adults. My mom, dad, and grandma died after prolonged illnesses the year Derek was born, 1989. I made as many three-thousand-mile trips as was feasible with a toddler, a newborn, and an overworked husband. Derek never cried once during those grueling trips from Spokane to Florida.

Many of those with autism become anxious when their routines are disrupted, as they find reassurance in knowing what their days will be like. I actually think that is true for all of us. I know that I don't function well without my daily to-do list. With Derek, though, it is a bit of a paradox; he loves to take trips with no idea where he will be going, but he becomes upset when his daily routine somehow goes awry. I have my usual routes around town, usually from one kid destination to another with errands to the bank, store, and post office in between. We live in a fairly small town, so I rarely get on the interstate unless I have to pick up someone from the airport. I think I'm single-handedly responsible for the ruts that are worn on Sprague Avenue, a main arterial in Spokane.

On a recent day I was running late to pick up Dylan, so I took the interstate to get across town more quickly. This must have meant "road trip" to Derek because when I got off on my exit, Derek started screaming and frantically kicking the back of my seat. I had to pull into a parking lot to give him medication and try to calm him down. He was truly devastated that he wasn't going on an adventure that included hotels and junk food. Instead, he had to endure the mundane task of hauling his brother home yet again.

We've had a few fiascos involving travel before Derek's medications made all our lives a bit more predictable, but for the most part, Derek is the best traveler of the bunch. He never gets bored or grumpy, and he can't ask, "Are we there yet?" He doesn't miss his friends because he doesn't have any. He loves buses, trains, plains, rental cars, boats, and on our most recent trip, helicopters and submarines.

Because all three kids attended school in different districts, it was rare that they had breaks at the same time. The exception was summer, so this is when we took most of our trips as a family. But in 2003, our family experienced a confluence of spring breaks except for Rex, so I planned a trip for the other four of us. I don't enjoy driving, so we discussed possible destinations arrived at by plane or boat. I think everyone thought I had finally lost it when I decided to take the kids on a Caribbean cruise that involved first flying from Washington State to Puerto Rico. My sanity was especially questioned by those who know that Derek cannot be trusted to ride the bus two miles to school. (The school district allows Derek to ride the bus only when I am with him because of past incidents when he became agitated.)

But aside from accidentally spewing hot decaf coffee all over an unsuspecting fellow traveler at the breakfast buffet, Derek behaved perfectly. When all he was expected to do was play in the water and visit the myriad buffets, he could not have been happier. Every day was filled with novel activities at various destinations. Derek even snorkeled on a coral reef. And when the rest of us were freaking out by a crazy taxi driver in Puerto Rico dodging in and out of traffic, Derek giggled approvingly. The weather was perfect, the islands we visited were beautiful, and we all had lots of fun.

Without any encouragement from anyone, Derek picked out a tacky straw hat on our first excursion and wore it the entire time we were gone. He was crestfallen when it blew off during our glass-bottom boat ride, but the nice captain was able to retrieve it for him. After that, it never left his head. In every picture I have from the trip, Derek is wearing his goofy hat. He hasn't, however, worn it once since we got home. His hat is for cruising and nothing else. This is a good example of how many individuals with autism are resistant to generalization.

Fish Trap

The following summer, on a weekend that Rex was on call, the kids talked me into taking them camping at a nearby lake called Fish Trap. Derek, who has always enjoyed water, giggled excitedly when he saw the lake and boarded the boat we rented with great enthusiasm. Whitney, Dylan, *and* Derek all caught their first fish—brim that were each a whopping four inches long. When we were back on land, Derek happily threw pebbles into the lake while Dylan and Whitney continued fishing on the dock. They all had fun setting up the tent and starting a campfire on their own. For dinner we had canned chili—heated right in the fire—and toasted marshmallows for desert. Dylan said it was the best dinner he ever had.

When it got dark, we sat snuggled in blankets telling ghost stories while Derek gazed at the crackling fire, mesmerized. It was a clear, beautiful night, and we were treated to a magnificent display:

the Perseid meteor shower. Away from the city lights, we could see a steady stream of meteors, large and small, streak across the night sky. When we finely crawled into our sleeping bags and closed up the tent, we could hear a little critter sniffing and scratching around the bottom of the tent, literally inches from our noses. It was probably a raccoon or a skunk, so I told everyone to lie perfectly still until it went away. In the distance we heard the mating calls of moose throughout the night.

The next morning we had Twinkies and Yoo-Hoos for breakfast as an eagle perched on the tree above us. Dylan said it was the best breakfast he ever had, and Derek nodded in agreement. I probably spent ten dollars on this wonderful, spur-of-the-moment outing. The kids weren't nearly as impressed with our Caribbean cruise that ended up costing almost five grand. The best memories often come from the most unexpected times.

Deep Six on Priest Lake

The last time Rex's family visited from Colorado, we rented a houseboat on one of the gorgeous mountain lakes in our area. There were areas where we could dock to enjoy the beaches and build campfires. The houseboat had a hot tub and a slide that delivered swimmers right into the lake. A large kitchen made it easy to keep the ever-hungry boaters fed.

We knew that Derek enjoyed dropping things in water to make a splash because of the always-present collection of objects at the bottom of our pool. During our three-day lake cruise, no one ever saw Derek doing anything untoward. But after we returned the boat and it was inspected for the return of our hefty security deposit, we were handed a lengthy list of "missing items" that added up to an amount significantly larger than our deposit. The list included various and sundry kitchen utensils, assorted tools and supplies, and even the upper-deck steering wheel, which Derek had evidently unbolted and flung overboard with no one noticing. Grandpa's fishing pole must have also fallen prey to our sneaky little flinger because it was gone when we unloaded. I think Derek must have enjoyed that lake cruise more than any of us.

Road Trips

When the kids were younger, I would homeschool them from time to time. We probably covered a hundred different study units that involved the entire family, including Derek in his own unique ways, immersing themselves in the topic of the month. We raised butterflies for the rain forest unit. We dissected a shark and went to SeaWorld for our marine biology unit. During our medieval unit, we had a madrigal feast for Rex's birthday and dressed Derek as the court jester. For the volcano unit, we visited all the volcanoes and lava flows in our state and made replicas of each. We visited the Grand Canyon, Bryce Canyon, Crater Lake, and Zion National Park for our geology unit. Derek turned out to be quite the little hiker. I couldn't come up with a geological reason for Circus Circus in Las Vegas, but we went anyway. We ate dinner at a Middle Eastern restaurant that had belly dancers as entertainment. Derek, age eleven at the time, usually doesn't react much to music, but he was really grooving to this beat and got a silly grin on his face when the dancer approached him. I got a great picture of him leering at her. Derek has never shown any sexual interest (praise Buddha), but this gal clearly tickled his fancy. I think it was the sparkly, jingly adornments of her ensemble that did it.

Probably the most memorable study unit was Native Americans. We made authentic clothes and moccasins out of deerskin, made our own pemmican, learned smoke signals and how to weave, and made a travois for our dog, Lucky. At the end of our study, we planned a trip to the Yakima reservation where we were going to camp in an "authentic" teepee and eat buffalo burgers. I had envisioned snuggly bearskins piled around a cozy fire, but when we entered our cool, authentic teepee, we found only bare concrete and no amenities whatsoever. I should not have assumed that there would at least be some cots or chairs. The only things we had in the way of gear were a cooler and Derek's beloved Sesame Street blanket—and we were in the middle of nowhere.

When I was deciding how I was going to make this work, Dylan ran up to me, saying he had an "owie." Evidently, he had mistaken a large, inclined, wooden ramp for a slide. I examined where the seat of his pants was torn and felt a three-inch-long splintered piece of wood deeply embedded in his left butt cheek. It had to come out, and he was pretty brave for the most part. I numbed the area with ice and used a pocketknife to cut a big enough opening to grab the piece of wood with a pair of vice grips from Rex's car. When I finally grabbed hold of it, Dylan started screaming, "*I don't want Daddy's tools in my butt!*" Dylan's distress quickly became Derek's, which in turn upset Whitney. As unrest ensued at the Porter powwow, I can only imagine what our fellow teepee-ers were thinking about this kooky family. Once I removed the wood, Dylan recovered and proudly showed his impressive trophy to everyone we came in contact with.

Rex found a store and brought back some juice, chips, and two bottles of wine. Despite Derek's displeasure, we spread his beloved blankie on the concrete and wadded up our sweatshirts for pillows. I was determined not to deprive my brood of this rich cultural experience. When our eyes had adjusted to the total darkness, small pairs of glowing bug eyes began appearing everywhere. Amazingly, the kids were all able to sleep. I, however, spent the night perched on the cooler with a shoe in my hand, planning our next study unit that was somehow going to include room service.

Chapter 13

SHOP 'TIL YA DROP

Rather that sitting in a hot car waiting for Dylan during all of his sports practices during recent summers, Derek and I would often walk in the mall—therapeutic for both Derek's mood and Mom's thighs. But on one fateful day, walking our routine laps at the Northtown Mall became anything but, as is usually the case with all things Derek. Derek was being especially well-mannered and good-natured, so I decided to reward his lack of aberrant behaviors with a quarter to use in a colorful candy machine of his choice. True to character, Derek went for the biggest candy, probably not understanding that he'd get more quantity with a smaller-sized candy. So he successfully produced what we both thought was a gigantic, orange gumball. He gleefully popped it into his mouth, and I heard the telltale tooth-cracking thud from his jaw. This was no gumball but a one-and-a-half-inch diameter jawbreaker. I didn't even think they made them anymore.

I immediately put my outstretched palm to Derek's mouth for him to spit the candy out. I caught the flicker of defiance in his eyes before I saw the gulp in his throat. He swallowed it whole—but not quite. His eyes got big and strangely bewildered, but not really afraid. Within seconds he was turning pink, and then red, and then blue. I screamed and threw my cell phone to a poor woman who was just passing by. I told her to call 911 as I climbed into a giant potted plant to make myself tall enough to attempt the

Heimlich maneuver. (At that time Derek was about five foot nine; I'm five feet.)

After a few failed attempts, I jumped out of the plant and dragged Derek to a bench. I bent him over the back of it, climbed on top of him, and pounded on his back. Brilliant orange, bubbly froth and drool bubbled from his mouth. I pleaded with the woman who had my phone to call Rex at work to see if he could think of anything to do before I had to open Derek's trachea with a pocketknife.

As this was transpiring, I was getting flashes of past emergencies I had been involved with—some had good endings, some did not. When I was in nursing school, a beloved instructor choked on a triangular-shaped cough drop. It lodged in her windpipe perfectly, blocking both branches of her airway. In a building full of trained medical professionals, there was nothing anyone could do. She was dead before the ambulance arrived. The paramedic who responded was her husband.

I was also involved with two patients who were unable to breathe and had to have tracheotomies before surgeons could arrive. Both, I'm happy to say, had good outcomes. I have witnessed enough to know that a person doesn't live long when the lungs don't receive air. In surgery, I saw countless children with various foreign bodies in their airways. If they made it to the operating room, they would usually be all right. I could not, however, remember any giant jawbreakers.

The woman who had my phone was able to reach Rex, who anxiously suggested that I try to get Derek to drink some water. He reasoned that the bubbling indicated some air was being expelled from the lungs; therefore, the jawbreaker was probably stuck in the esophagus and only partially blocking the trachea. That large of an object, though, could still impinge on the airway, compromising breathing. Rex thought that water might help lubricate and dissolve the jawbreaker, helping it slide down the esophagus.

Mall security arrived on scene and helpfully provided cups of water, paper towels, and moral support. Derek was as calm as I was hysterical. Most of the water he tried to drink came right back out, but enough must have found its way down. After what seemed like an eternity, Derek's chest heaved and an audible gulp escaped his throat. He managed to swallow, and his normal coloration was quickly restored. The jawbreaker must have melted enough for it to slide down the esophagus.

I think the worst part of the ordeal for Derek, aside from the barrage of maternal assaults he endured, was when the jawbreaker again got stuck at the cardiac sphincter, which is the muscular opening of the stomach. Derek showed signs of discomfort for quite a few minutes while the candy colossus sat at this juncture. He then exhibited a painful grimace, followed by palpably relaxed relief. When the ambulance finally arrived, Derek was very orange and pretty wet, but okay. The shoppers at Northtown Mall got quite a show that day. There will be no encores, God willing.

Chapter 14

BLOOD AND BEGONIAS

It was the mother of bad mornings. I almost never get sick, but when I do, I get very sick. I woke up with a pounding headache and an unquenchable thirst. The kids were nine, seven, and four, and two of them were standing by my bed when I was mustering up the courage to open my eyes. I made it downstairs and had a breakfast of two cans of Diet Pepsi and three aspirins. The thermometer read 103.4. I thanked God that it was summer and that carpool was not on the day's agenda. Whitney helped feed her brothers Cheerios, and then went upstairs to get dressed. Derek went out on the back deck to play, and Dylan used my weakened state to plop in front of the brain-sucker for a marathon cartoon session.

I was about to lie on the couch when the phone rang: a cold call from a stockbroker with all kinds of recommendations for me. I was about to inform him of my disinterest now or in the future when I happened to look through the sliding glass door and see Derek munching on the begonias just like a billy goat would. At the same time Derek began to vomit, Whitney came staggering down the stairs, covered in blood. When Dylan saw her he began screaming uncontrollably. "Blood and puke—gotta go!"

I threw down the phone and picked up Whitney, who was on the verge of fainting. I laid her on the floor and grabbed a dishtowel to soak up enough blood to determine how badly she was hurt. I found a large gash through her left eyebrow—not too serious, but it would definitely need stitches. She told me she walked into a wall.

I brought Derek in when he was through covering the deck with pink and yellow vomit. When we discovered Derek's propensity for pica, or cravings for abnormal things to eat, we researched all of the plants in our yard and removed any that were toxic. Only the rhizomes of some begonias are mildly toxic. Still, I called poison control to be double-check and was reassured. I guess begonias just didn't agree with Derek.

I called Rex, but he was still in surgery. I called a neighbor, briefly explained my situation, and asked whether she could take Whitney to the emergency room so I could stay with the boys. She said she could if I would watch the dog of her friend who was visiting (who happened to be Whitney's second-grade teacher). She didn't tell me it was a sweet but territorial, giant Great Dane. My dog, Lucky, a corgi/lab mix, was equally sweet—and territorial. The two barked at each other the entire time Whitney was getting sewn up—almost as loudly as Dylan screamed. He was convinced that his sister had died. I finally calmed Dylan and reassured him that his sister would be returning home "as good as new." After Derek recovered from his rather bizarre breakfast, he popped in a favorite video to watch, unbothered by the surrounding cacophony. By the time Whitney was done at the hospital, her dad was able to bring her home. I crawled up the stairs to our bedroom and locked the door.

Chapter 15

MOMENTUM AND IMPULSE

When Derek was about four or five, he went through what we refer to as his Galilean phase. Our deck was his leaning tower of Pisa. Any chance he got, he would find something—preferably breakable—sail it off of the deck, and gleefully giggle as it smashed onto the concrete. Glasses became his favorite, and soon the only "glassware" remaining in our cupboard was Solo cups. Coffee cups were next, and then plates. Finally, the dishwasher sat idle for months, so I stored bread and chips in it. No consequences could dissuade Derek from his gravitational gallivanting. His favorite Christmas gift was the tree because it was filled with colorful missiles that made a distinctive and satisfying "pop" on impact.

During this phase, when we stayed in an Orlando hotel, we were getting dressed to go out to eat and none of us could find our shoes. Derek had dropped them off the balcony and into the bushes three stories down. Our trips to Mexico and Priest Lake were during this phase of momentum and impulse and showed distinct elements of both. During the summer when the pool was open, he scoured the yard for rocks to plop into the deep end.

At Derek's elementary school, his classroom window was right next to the entrance of the building. As one who knew Derek might expect, a collection of various and sundry items were always piled on the ground below the window. Inside the classroom, the depository of choice was behind the refrigerator. Derek preferred elevated platforms from which to test the effects of matter and gravity, but he would satisfy his compulsion by shifting to tests of visual-spatial capacity when on ground zero. He achieved this by cramming assorted items into nooks and crannies that would accommodate them

I occasionally come across assorted Derek deposits from years past, but he no longer seems to have this obsession. I think the medication (risperidone) he took helped with the OCD that is part of his autism.

Chapter 16

NEVER A DULL MOMENT

Recently Derek and I were running errands after we left his high school. From the backseat, Derek reached up to give me the sign for "toilet" for the fourteenth time as I was driving through town, trying to think of somewhere that had a bathroom. I signed "just a minute" to him yet again. Derek started screaming and kicking the back of my seat. I was stopped at a red light, and a sheriff's deputy pulled up next to me. I heard the seat belt unbuckle and turned to find Derek kneeling in the backseat with his pants down and his penis in a Gatorade bottle. I grabbed the bottle and said, "*No!* Not here, not now!"

Derek has normal bladder control but not normal patience; he does not like to be put off. The deputy was thankfully attending to his computer and seemed oblivious to the scene on his left. I was grateful, too, for the tinting in the rear windows of my car. I was just about to exhale when I heard an explosion in the backseat. The left rear window of the car was shattered, and glass was everywhere. Derek sat stunned. At first I thought we were being shot at, and then realized that Derek had punched out the window in anger. The deputy never even looked over at us. The light mercifully turned green. The new window cost $350. Derek peed at Kmart.

Welcome Home, Whit

When Whitney flew home from college last Thanksgiving, Rex let Dylan drive with his new learner's permit and took Derek along for the ride so I could stay home and do some cooking. When they got home, Derek was wild-eyed, Dylan was as white as a sheet, Whitney was in tears, and Rex was shaking his head. All that I could get out of Whitney was: "First, Derek tried to kill me. Then, Dylan tried to kill me."

Rex explained that when Derek realized he was at the airport to pick up his sister rather than embark on a vacation of his own, he went berserk in the car. Dylan swerved into the oncoming lane, and then quickly overcorrected driving the car into a culvert, nearly rolling it. If Whitney chooses to spend her next break in Cancun, I won't blame her.

I wish there was a way to make Derek understand that it is because of these behaviors that he is no longer able to travel with us the way he previously did. With the correct drug regimen, he might be fine on an airline flight, but we're not willing to risk it at this point. I just heard on the news that a flight was canceled because of the tantrum of a two-year-old toddler. This seems like an overreaction to me, but there is a lot less tolerance for misbehavior during travel with the heightened awareness for terrorism in recent years.

Chapter 17

MICE, METRICS, AND McDONALD'S

My eyes popped open one recent morning at about 2:30 AM. Getting to sleep used to be my problem, now I also have trouble staying asleep—I am fifty, and it is probably a symptom of menopause. I don't fight it; I embrace it. It allows me periods of quiet solitude to read, write, or watch an old movie undisturbed.

On the same morning, I was poring through articles I had researched and printed. I have a brain that craves constant stimulation, whether from a crossword puzzle, an obscure article on something I know nothing about, a new recipe on the Food Network, or learning tai chi. I'm fairly easily entertained and rarely bored.

The problem is that by the time everyone else is emerging, I'm thinking that sleeping until noon sounds pretty good. Of course, that's not an option and so the morning routine begins. Rex now gives Derek his morning meds before he leaves for work so that the medication has a chance to kick in before Derek and Dylan get up at 6:30 AM (working well so far). Derek either goes back to sleep awhile or comes upstairs and watches a DVD. After I kiss Rex good-bye, I make a pot of Derek's favorite herbal tea so he can start the day on a happy note. Derek's morning routine is broken down on his AM schedule, which lists all the steps of grooming and dressing. He has become so independent in this regard that he rarely needs to consult his schedule anymore.

When Derek woke up, he happily bounded up the stairs and

offered no resistance to the insistent pace needed to get out the door on time—a welcome response. We promptly delivered Dylan to his high school at 7:30 and made it across town in time for Derek's morning reading session with Michele at the elementary school. As agreed upon as a safety precaution, we have to be finished by 8:30 before the younger students begin arriving. Derek seemed eager to be there, but I sensed some anxiety. I think he likes being able to read, but it is still taxing for him. The OCD behaviors kicked in as soon as we entered the classroom: closing all the drawers and cabinets tightly, closing all the mini-blinds, putting school supplies away, stuffing poofed-up tissues back into their boxes, and in general, straightening and tidying the classroom. He then began signing for coffee and pretzels, his present rewards for successful work sessions at school, which I have let get out of hand. In the kitchen area of the classroom, I make him "Derek Mocha": watered-down decaf and leftover chocolate milk from the previous day's lunch. I drag the process out as long as possible—a stall tactic to allow him to get some work done. If he knows I'm meeting his request, he won't stress and is better able to concentrate. During our time there, I try to limit him to two cups.

It was nearing the end of his last school year, and I sensed that he was getting restless. I didn't have high expectations when he met with Michele because of his mildly agitated state. However, I was surprised at how focused and attentive he was during their session. He did some reading and got through his entire stack of 125 sight words, though with less accuracy than usual. Even though he was exhibiting "that edginess," I was happy and relieved at how well he held it together—probably in response to his new medication regimen. I had forgotten his pretzels and only had crackers to offer as rewards instead. On any other day this could have been grounds for distress, but though clearly displeased and somewhat disgruntled, Derek reluctantly ate them.

So the session lasted a slightly stressful, yet successful thirty minutes when he stood up, put the materials away, and signed out. He wanted to go out to the playground, where he joyfully and frenetically swung for twenty-five minutes, as though it was satisfying a vestibular craving. When he was done, it was 9:00 AM and we had an hour and a half before showing up at the high school. Derek doesn't like to eat breakfast first thing in the morning, so we use this time to go to the grocery store and shop for a healthy morning meal—usually an apple, some juice, and a deli sandwich or salad. He picked only an apple and a diet pop this day, which I knew wasn't going to fill him up, so I decided to give him a rare treat: breakfast at McDonald's. A large shade tree in the parking lot made it a pleasant place for Derek to eat. When I cracked the window, an audible hissing immediately got my attention. Freon? Nope, left front tire—flat within seconds.

My dad and I rebuilt my five-hundred-dollar 1965 Mustang when I was in high school, so I think of myself as fairly mechanically inclined. I can change my own oil and have no problem changing a tire—or so I thought. I would much rather get my hands dirty than wait up to an hour for roadside service to appear.

I unloaded the spare, jack, and "jack tools" and discovered a giant nest of mice in the storage compartment. I knew there were mice in the car because of the little presents they had been leaving me. My husband had trapped four of them, but some persistent relations were still camped out in my hatchback.

I put the jack in place and loosened the lug nuts of the wheel. Then, I remembered that the set of wheels had an antitheft fifth lug nut that required a socket adapter. I phoned my husband, who thought the adapter was in the glove box—which it was—and I was one lug nut from being on my way. However, while the adapter fit the lug nut, the lug wrench did not fit the adapter.

Fortunately, an automotive store was right next to where we were parked at McDonald's. I attempted to buy an adapter for the adapter, but to no avail. A Good Samaritan who came by told me that he thought it was stripped, until he realized that the adapter was metric while the lug wrench was standard. I like being able to take care of myself and don't take well to the role of damsel in distress; however, when my Eagle Scout dressed down the auto store employees and found a lug wrench that worked, I was very grateful. I canceled the call for roadside assistance and offered to buy the breakfasts of my wrench rescuer and his mom. He refused and said to "pay it forward"—nice guy.

Because this tire fiasco had taken almost two hours and Derek already missed lunch, there was no point in going to high school now. Besides, Derek was probably full from all of the fast food I was feeding him while he patiently took in our parking lot debacle.

We finally hobbled on the spare to the tire store about five miles away and were told there was an hour wait to have the tire repaired—not a huge problem for me, but for Derek on a new medication regimen, a distinct unknown. We sat in the car for a half hour until the mechanics were ready to work on it. Fortunately or unfortunately, right next to the seating area the tire store offered lukewarm, sludgy coffee with sugar and trans-fat–laden, nondairy creamer. Derek immediately began signing "coffee" before he even sat down. I said okay and slowly made a small cup for him, which he chugged immediately. I tried to cajole him into taking a walk outside, but he flatly refused and instead insisted on more coffee. Derek obsesses on highly desired items as long as they are in plain sight. The last thing I needed then was Derek jacked up on a ten-cup caffeine jag. For these types of unforeseen situations, I usually have an emergency stash of distracters—sugarless candy or apples—and today was no different. What also helped was a copy of *Auto Trader* that Derek happened to fixate on for a time. My stall tactics and some additional meds worked to keep him down to only three half-cups of coffee and a handful of candy.

Thankfully, we survived this potentially stressful morning without incident. It was a beautiful spring day and when we got home, we walked and skipped up and down our long driveway—happy to be home.

Chapter 18
NONVERBAL

A small clicking sound came from under the familiar blue comforter. (Derek's sign for "peanut" is to click his thumbnail against his front teeth.) I dutifully went to the pantry for the jar of peanuts. A hand emerged from a corner of the comforter, palm up and Thing-like (think Addams Family). When full of peanuts, the palm closed and withdrew into its dark origin. The clicking was replaced with muffled munching for a minute or two, and then the clicking began again. This could have gone on until I had emptied the jar, but it didn't. When I told him "Enough already," the clicking was replaced by irritated whining. This is an example of how Derek currently communicates.

Derek did have some language when he was little, but none that was functional after about age four. He now has about twenty signs and pictures he uses to request food, but I think it is safe to say that the jury is no longer out: Derek is nonverbal. It is not for lack of trying. He received very early intervention therapy from the most respected professionals in the country, whom I still greatly respect. Their proven methods just did not resonate with Derek. In all of the years of therapy, speech therapists also did not make much difference . Any success they did have was through behavioral interventions, such as ABA (applied behavioral analysis) and DTT (discrete trial training).

Early on—ages three to five—the PECS (picture exchange communication system) worked well for us. At the time, it consisted of a loose-leaf binder with pages of Velcro-attached icons and pictures of things Derek commonly requested. I still use variations of this approach today. For example, I made a picture menu of all the lunch selections at the high school so that Derek can order his lunch independently. He is also required to sign "please" and "thank you" to the friendly lunchroom staff. Food is the main motivator for Derek, so I milk it for everything it's worth. His DDD (Department of Developmental Disability) caseworker and current speech pathologist at his high school have been helpful in trying to obtain a portable personal communicator, which would allow for Derek to communicate, even with those who know no sign language. The personal communicator is a computer that can be programmed with everything Derek might request or wish to "say," and it displays an array of words or pictures. When he touches the chosen icon, the device will produce an audible sentence for him.

But for now, Derek has communication notebooks with hundreds of pictures that he uses to communicate. In one book that we keep in the kitchen, the majority of the pictures are of food items and utensils. There are also pictures of his favorites: his room, the bathroom, his chariot, the trampoline, and the pool. Derek uses this book the most; he flips through the pages and points to what he would like to request. I try to keep on hand all the items in the book, so he doesn't become frustrated when I am unable to provide what he requests. If I run out of an item, I try to remember to temporarily remove the picture from the book. It is best to keep "treat choices" separate, as most kids won't make healthy choices when their array includes candy or dessert items. When the child earns a treat, offer pictures of three different items to choose from and then put the pictures away, so that they cannot become fixated on them.

Communication book

The communication book I keep in my car contains pictures of common daily or weekly destinations, including school, the post office, grocery store, mall, gas station, car wash, YMCA, and various restaurants we frequent. I also have a stack of pictures for infrequent destinations such as the doctor, dentist, hospital, and airport. I point to the pictures to inform Derek of where we are going or what we will be doing. Sometime we will still "picture argue"—I point to where we will be going (school), and he points to where he would prefer to go (the grocery store). Even when he doesn't get his way, he is usually compliant because at least he was able to "voice" his opinion. Over the years, I have learned that nearly all of the behaviors that those with autism exhibit are born of frustration from not being able to make needs, or wants, known.

Derek's latest method of communication is actually quite direct. He loves chili, so a couple of times a day he will bring me a can of chili, a bowl, a spoon, and the can opener. I could teach him to use a can opener but don't, because his need for help is an opportunity for communication and interaction. When he wants something, he has to request it by either by giving me a picture of what he wants, bringing me his empty bowl when he wants more of what he was eating, or signing what he would like. If Derek were completely independent in our home, he would rarely interact with anyone. I also haven't taught him to use the microwave, stove, or toaster for the same reason, and also because of safety issues such as burns, fire, or electric shock.

I've also found elements of Robert Koegel's book *Teaching Pivotal Behaviors* to be helpful throughout the years. When Derek was first diagnosed, I called Dr. Koegel, a renowned autism specialist. It must have been after-hours, but he happened to still be in his office and picked up the phone. (He and his wife are frequent speakers at conferences on autism. I have found their lectures and books, especially *Teaching Children with Autism*, to be very helpful.) I described Derek to him briefly, and he told me to simply "talk to Derek." For example, when I put him to bed, I was to tell him what we'd be doing tomorrow, using simple, familiar language: "Tomorrow is swimming." Dr. Koegel assured me that my son understood more than he appeared to. I wasn't convinced at first but soon noticed that each night, Derek began to wait for me to tell him what tomorrow would bring. It lessens his anxiety when he knows what to expect, which is typical of children with autism. They need routine and need to be warned about departures from their normal schedules. Cardboard strips with Velcro and attached icons and written or visual schedules are again helpful in this regard.

Currently, four boys in Derek's academic (as opposed to vocational) classroom have autism. They all present, however, very differently; each has his own unique strengths and problems. They are all in their mid-to-late teens and communicate in completely different ways. Mark and Derek are the poster kids for autism. They have each and every characteristic on the DSM (Diagnostic and Statistical Manual) checklist. Mark is nonverbal and uses a Vantage, an electronic augmentative speech device, similar to the one ordered for Derek, to communicate. When he pushes an icon from the display, an electronic voice "speaks" for him. When he needs to use the bathroom, he pushes the toilet icon and the device says, "I need to use the bathroom."

What is "said" for each icon is programmable and the icons can be organized by categories or alphabetically for easy access. His academic skills and understanding of routine are superior to Derek's. He is quick to correct his teacher when there is even the slightest departure from the day's routine. The other day, after reviewing the day's schedule upon arriving, Mark walked to the other side of the room and chose an icon from a large array of choices. The untrained observer would probably assume that this action was random, but they would be wrong; Mark was on a mission. After reading the schedule for the day—hang up your backpack, wash your hands, get your breakfast, complete your assignment, swimming, lunch, class activity, leisure activity choice, bus home—he was distressed. It was Friday, and once a month on Friday, we go to the mall for lunch at the food court. Wendy's is a popular choice for this group. Mark had picked the Wendy's icon to add to the schedule (which, in his mind, was incomplete). He was unhappy to learn that this was a no-Wendy's Friday. Also a techno kid, Mark is well attuned to computers and his Game Boy.

Derek, on the other hand, couldn't be any less interested in anything technological unless it can cook him food. He has shown glimmers of interest in one school computer game of late and will now "ask" for coffee using an old communicator donated by a previous student. (When Derek pushes the button that has an icon for coffee, a mechanized recording plays requesting coffee.) Our main goals for summer school will be trying to pique these new interests and hopefully expand on them.

Jessie is a gorgeous young man with a photographic memory. He is verbal, but his speech is largely echolalic (he simply repeats back what is said to him, like an "echo") and not very functional. He is the only one who has strong math skills of the four.

Bobby has fragile-X syndrome (a chromosomal abnormality that is definitively diagnosed by a blood test), which is now considered an autism spectrum disorder. He has the most functional speech but is painfully shy and socially ill at ease. Each student has a different curriculum customized with work and activities at his specific level in each study area. From my observations over the years, it is striking to see how different these young men really are.

Because those with autism can present in myriad ways, it is important to try all kinds of ways to reinforce communication and to reintroduce various methods at different intervals. Something that was not effective at one point might all of a sudden click at another point. As stated previously, Derek recently had this experience. At age eighteen, after years of trials, Derek had an explosion of sight-word recognition that has grown into sentence construction and reading. During the last school year, Derek went from a five-word "vocabulary" to a 125-word "vocabulary."

For younger children, Dr. Stanley Greenspan's method of interaction, called "floor play," might work well. At the age when autistic children seem to be most withdrawn (ages two to five), it is helpful to sit on the floor with them and imitate what they do (even if it's "stimming"—self-stimulating behaviors such as hand-flapping, finger-flicking, spinning, and rocking) and try to make eye contact and a connection, using their choice of activity. When Derek was first diagnosed, we traveled across the state of Washington to the University of Washington so Derek could receive therapy in Dr. Geraldine Dawson's toddler program for children with autism. She was implementing interventions similar to Dr. Greenspan's and Derek responded well. His eye contact improved, and he became more engaged.

Today

I am at peace with Derek's inability to speak; I believe it is because we communicate so well. Derek and I are like an old married couple who knows what the other is going to "say" before that person does. Derek's communication consists mainly of a steady stream of signs requesting food items. Usually they come four at a time: peanut, cookie, coffee, tea. This actually translates into "Feed me, I'm hungry."

My communication to him is usually barking orders like a drill sergeant: "Take a bath." "Shoes on." "Let's go." "Go swim." "Clothes in washer." Simple, clear, familiar, direct language works best. Too many conjunctions, modifiers, and adjectives are too hard to process. I usually sign what I'm saying as well as speak it aloud. Since Derek's recent increase in sight-word vocabulary, I also write down for him anything he asks for before giving it to him.

At his most verbal, Derek pokes up his extended index fingers excitedly and says, "Pop, pop, pop." He is signing and requesting "popcorn." We were recently greeted with this exuberant display upon returning from a rare dinner out. Dylan was watching him and extracted this rare vocalization just goofing around with Derek. Fifteen years of speech therapy hasn't been as successful. The next day at school, Derek made more attempts at speech. He added "ple" (please), "ba" (ball), "coff" (coffee), and "cow."

We are more bewildered than elated at this newly established repertoire because these mini-breakthroughs are often fleeting. In fact, these attempts were not established at all; we haven't heard them again. Parents of autistic children are often told (as I was) that if the child isn't talking by age five to seven, he or she most likely won't. They may also be told that early inquisitiveness and curiosity are the best indicators of future success with job and life skills. Derek had neither of these, except at about eighteen months old, he would ask "What's that? What's that?"

Acceptance of a life dependent on and protected by me came with peace after years of battles with his autism. I'm probably one of the most stubborn people you'll ever meet, but I'm also an informed realist. It isn't that I've given up on improvement in Derek's communication; it is just that I now have to focus on what Derek is most going to benefit from at this point in his life. It is after I can no longer provide this comfort zone for Derek that I worry. He is way too dependent on me, and I know it. Our current situation, which has me acting as his aide at school, isn't helping either. During his transition from high school into the community in some capacity, he will have to learn to be more independent. This will hopefully come from a skilled behavior and job-skills coach that I haven't met yet. His caseworker at the Department of Vocational Rehabilitation is currently planning for that. After high school, I am guardedly optimistic and know that we'll have to wait and see. But I'm used to that.

Is nonverbal such a bad thing? Most people with teen-agers would say no! Of course, I wish Derek had useful language, but if he were only able to say rather that sign the things on which he obsesses, I'd probably lose my mind. I'm not one for idle chatter and prefer that those who don't have anything important to say refrain from speaking. Derek asking me for peanuts and coffee four hundred times a day would definitely put me over the edge. But for Derek to be able to tell me that his head hurts or that he loves me … I would sacrifice just about anything.

Dreaded Appointments

Visits to doctors' and dentists' offices can be especially trying for children with autism and their parents. Starting as young as possible with careful planning and preparation can alleviate much of the stress associated with these necessary appointments. Letting the child with autism accompany his siblings during their appointments, if possible, will increase the child's familiarity with the surroundings and procedures. Even if it is not evident how much receptive language the child has, describe to the child in simple language about where he'll be going and what he will experience. Using actual pictures is helpful in this regard. After getting permission, I took pictures of the office building, hospital, exam room, dental chair, equipment, scales, and anything I thought my son would encounter. From those photographs, I made *The Doctor Book* and *The Dentist Book* and added simple captions. For the week prior to the appointment, Derek and I read the book together and took it with us to the appointment to prepare for each step of the experience. I have been fortunate with Derek's dental health; I have used the Sonicare toothbrush for his dental hygiene with impressive results. Derek has had no cavities, and so the dentist visits have been mostly trauma free. I'm fairly certain that if any drilling became necessary, we would need to use general anesthesia.

Having outgrown general pediatric visits, doctor's appointments are rare because Derek is seldom ill. However, with his current medication, annual blood work is required. Given Derek's history of aggressive behaviors, especially when he is anxious, I was dreading his latest blood draw. In preparation, I played phlebotomist with him when he was in a good mood. I tied rubber tubing around his arm and gently poked him with a needleless syringe. I had Rex bring home some EMLA from the hospital for the day of Derek's appointment; this is an anesthetizing ointment that is applied to the skin of the draw site about thirty minutes before blood is drawn. Rex and I both accompanied him to the hospital lab with fingers crossed. I applied the tourniquet and held his extended arm while blocking his view of the procedure. Rex stood behind him and distracted him with candy. The technician was successful on the first poke and filled four vials of blood in record time. Derek never even flinched. The results of the blood work were normal.

During his recent physical examination, Derek was also completely cooperative and tolerated it all exceptionally well. All of my worry was for naught.

Chapter 19

TRANSITION

Derek is now in what is referred to as *transition,* the period at the end of high school between the ages of eighteen and twenty-one. He is considered graduated but will still attend high school for three more years. During this time he will receive vocational training to prepare him for employment when he leaves school and enters the workforce in the community. The Department of Vocational Rehabilitation and the high school work together in this regard. Derek is in priority category 1: individuals with the most severe disabilities. He has already been evaluated for recommendations for possible job placement. We are now waiting to hear what options the team will suggest.

During this transition period, rather than sitting in a classroom, Derek has been encouraged to try out different "jobs" and vocational skills; this will help his case workers find an appropriate placement for him when the transition period is over. I was skeptical that this was going to work for Derek, but after hearing several successful accounts, I am guardedly optimistic.

One such account that impressed me was in the 2007 first edition of the *Autism Advocate,* a magazine published by the Autism Society of America five times each year. The article, "Off to Work for Individuals with Autism," describes a young woman with behavior problems similar to and even more severe than Derek's. With a full-time behavior-support specialist/job coach, she is successfully employed and is living independently in a group home with support staff. During her transition, her family took advantage of the Social Security program PASS (Plan to Achieve Self Support.) This program allows a portion of her earnings to pay for her job coach but not to be counted against her eligibility for Social Security income (SSI) or other benefits. She then moved to IRWE (impairment related work expense), which is intended for people with disabilities who require ongoing support to continue working while paying as much of the cost for this support program as they can. She and her job coach pay more in taxes than she gets in SSI and food stamps. In the article, her parents stress the importance of gearing a child with autism toward gainful employment well before graduation. I am truly inspired by this determined family; they have given me hope for similar success.

There is an excellent free publication put out by the National Information Center for Children and Youth with Disabilities (NICHCY) titled *Vocational Assessment* (www.nichcy.org/pubs/ outprint/ts6txt.htm). It is applicable to high school students who are in transition and includes several suggestions for parents, listed in the summary (page 14), that would be helpful in meeting the student's needs during the transition stage.

I now have to navigate the bureaucracies that Derek will depend on when I am no longer here to care for and protect him. I realize how important it is to have all of this in place, and while I take this responsibility seriously, I still hate it. Most of the people I have dealt with are well-intentioned and helpful, but I have not had this experience with those at the Social Security Administration in DC. They have been rude, uncaring, and uninformed and have given me the wrong information more often than not. I have been repeatedly put on hold for durations of up to forty minutes. If I questioned the information I was being given, they just hung up.

Derek has finally been approved and is receiving benefits, so now my contact with the SSI folks will be mercifully limited.

While literally drowning in the alphabet soup that is now my life, Derek was assigned a Washington Department of Developmental Disability (DDD) caseworker, who became my life preserver. She sent me packets of information, all the necessary forms she said I needed, and even a DVD that spelled out in plain English the purposes of all the different agencies that I need to access on Derek's behalf. I still feel like I'm treading water, but at least I can intermittently surface for air. I have applied for Medicaid for Derek in the hope that it will help defray the cost of his meds, which now run about $1,100 a month. I have also applied to become Derek's "care provider," so that a stranger isn't assigned to fill that role. As an RN, I qualify without the mandatory training and am still able to take care of all of Derek's needs. Also, I have had several negative experiences with home health-care workers. I know that many good ones exist, but I have been unlucky.

When hospice was caring for my mom, and my father was also terminally ill, the workers stole and used my parents' credit cards and cleaned out their checking account. Several thousands of dollars worth of charges appeared on their accounts. It took me months to get their finances restored. I also have had money and jewelry stolen from my home by caretakers, so I am reluctant to have respite care for Derek in my home. I am told that there are places where Derek could be cared for on a limited basis, like a group home that offers temporary placements. However, Derek wouldn't be able to tell me if anyone mistreated him, and I wouldn't trust someone I didn't know well to properly care for him.

Guardianship

The whole concept of guardianship has annoyed me since learning that is the only legal way to take care of Derek's affairs since he turned eighteen. He came out of my body, and I have literally devoted my life to caring for him since birth. I understand that safeguards are needed to protect those who are taken advantage of or unable to care for themselves. It just seems arbitrarily ironic to me that one day Rex and I are solely responsible for Derek's entire being, and the next day we have no legal authority or responsibility whatsoever.

Recently, I had to take classes and hire attorneys, at a cost of two thousand dollars, so a judge could look at our obviously safe and caring situation and declare that I can be Derek's guardian. I wanted so badly to ask him just what he thought I had been doing for the past eighteen years, but I didn't. I'm sure he would have told me of the countless poorly cared-for wards of the state who had no one to look out for them.

So it is now official: I am Derek's guardian. And if someone drops a house on me, the honor will go to my husband. During the process of the guardianship, we were given background checks and our home was inspected. The court-appointed guardian came to our home and asked us numerous questions about how Derek is cared for and what his limitations are. We were asked to leave the room at one point so the attorney could ask Derek about his concerns. Rex and I knowingly glanced at each other and smiled. "Okey dokey," I said.

We giggled in the kitchen and poked our heads around the corner to watch "the interview." The attorney asked Derek whether he had any reservations about his mother becoming his guardian. Derek signed, "Gum."

The attorney asked Derek whether he had been mistreated in anyway. Derek signed, "Apple."

The attorney asked Derek whether he would prefer to live in a group home. Derek signed, "Candy."

"Okay, Mrs. Porter, I think I've gotten sufficient information."

Yeah, like establishing that Derek is really hungry.

Okay, so here it all is:

- SSI—check
- DSHS (Department of Social and Health Services)/ DDD—check
- DVR—check
- GAU/GAX (General Assistance Unemployable/and medical coverage)—pending
- Medicaid—pending
- Care provider—pending
- Guardianship—check
- SSI-designated payee account (a joint bank account of the recipient and his or her guardian)—check
- SSI/PASS/IRWE-supported employment—fingers crossed.

Navigating through these different agencies made me feel like a rat in maze or the steel ball in a pinball machine. When I initially applied for DDD approval for Derek (this is the lion at the gate through which all other benefits are accessed), the agency misfiled his information for seven months. I had to repeat the applications process and produce copies (which I thankfully had) of everything I had already submitted. The next agency scolded me for my tardiness. I remember during one of the intake appointments, I was in a DVR office thinking I was in a DDD office. Why I was there, I'm still not sure. At any rate, I have dutifully filled out any form that has come my way, even if I don't know why. I figured someone sent it for a reason that I probably wouldn't understand even if they explained it.

Derek began receiving his Social Security checks in March, but I had nowhere to deposit them until the guardianship was approved at the end of May. It is illegal to commingle any funds, so Derek has to have a separate checking account. He cannot, however, open an account because he is unable to endorse his checks. Even as his SSI-designated payee, I cannot be a cosigner on his nonexistent account until I have power of attorney. I was informed by the lawyer I was forced to hire that the guardianship that was about to be approved trumped power of attorney, making power of attorney redundant. So his checks sat in a pile until I got a paper from the legal wizards saying, "*POOF!* You're a guardian."

I was planning on depositing every penny Derek received into a life trust for when he is no longer dependent on his dad and me, but now as a guardian, I have to keep meticulous records of his income and expenses. A bank account provides a paper trail for the court that I must report to annually. I again realize the potential for abuse, but I am still annoyed. We are required to charge Derek rent and living expenses because if his personal funds exceed two thousand dollars, his benefits will cease. So basically, we are laundering money so I can give Derek all the funds he receives. I receive his SS check as designated payee. I endorse it as "Approved Account Signer" and deposit it into Derek's account. Then I write a check from Derek's account to myself for rent and living expenses so money doesn't accumulate in his account over the restricted limit. Finally, I deposit that check into our checking account and write a check to deposit in Derek's life-trust account, as the money in the trust account doesn't count toward the two thousand dollar limit. Welcome to the world of government bureaucracies! It would be funny if it wasn't so maddeningly ridiculous.

Chapter 20

TRANSFERENCE

The following are opinions from a mom who wants answers just as badly as anyone else who has a loved one with autism. No one wants to hear that autism is incurable or lifelong. But at this point, the real, not imagined or desired, information is what allows us to best deal with autism.

Autism is truly the worst thing that has ever happened to my family, and we have not led sheltered lives. Both my husband and I grew up in low-income, blue-collar families. Yet we were all smart, hardworking people who were determined to make better lives for ourselves and our future families. Rex and I are the only ones who went to college in our families. We are now living the American dream, which happens to include the nightmare of autism. I am so empathetic to families with limited means who are trying to deal with this unimaginable encroachment on their lives; so many of the therapies available are quite costly as well as exhausting. In addition, a responsive school district is imperative for helping families with early intervention when autism is even suspected.

I am fascinated with the neurobiology of autism and have found Margaret Bauman and Thomas Kemper's book *The Neurobiology of Autism* to be an excellent resource. I attended a seminar in which Margaret Bauman presented. (She is an associate clinical professor of neurology at Harvard Medical School.) I frantically took notes as though I was in a college course that I was about to fail. Her irrefutable research brought me such peace in truly understanding what actually was wrong with my son. After her lecture and my own follow-up research, I was convinced that the developing brain of those who develop autism is impacted early in utero. There may be some as yet unconfirmed environmental triggers, such as pesticides, plastic components such as bispenol-A and phthalates and other industrial pollution or infections, working in concert with a genetic predisposition for autism. Bauman covered areas needing further study, such as genetics, neurochemistry, neuroanatomy, pathology and embryology.

The evidence of the timing of the early stages of embryological development was especially illuminating to me, as the emerging information strongly suggests that autism happens early in the prenatal period. The research continues, and more answers as well as more questions will be forthcoming. I believe further studies will eventually conclude that there are probably several types of autism with multiple combinations of causes.

The 2007 report from the Centers for Disease Control—which can be found on its Web site, www.cdc.gov/ncbddd/autism/)—estimates that about 1 in 150 eight-year-old children in the United States have an autism spectrum disorder (ASD). The male-to-female ratio has remained at about four to one. When Derek was diagnosed in 1991, the incidence of being diagnosed with autism was about 1 in 2,500. This apparent marked increase probably represents an increased awareness leading to more diagnoses and a large increase in what is being included on the much-expanded spectrum. Other diagnoses currently included on that spectrum are Asperger's syndrome, childhood disintegrative disorder, Rett syndrome, a percentage of those with fragile-X syndrome, and pervasive developmental disorder, not otherwise specified (PPD-NOS). Whatever the true prevalence is, the perceived increase has enhanced awareness and positively impacted the funding for research.

Infantile or classical autism (as it was referred to in the past) or regressive or low-functioning autism (as it is sometimes currently categorized) is the most common condition on the autism disorder spectrum. It is identified by the time the child is fourteen months old and is characterized by deficits in communication, impaired social abilities, narrow or obsessive interests, and often repetitive, self-stimulating behaviors that stem from sensory integration difficulties.

Because there are no specific tests or known biological markers that exist for autism, it is difficult to definitively diagnose. For this reason, the American Psychiatric Association developed a definition and list of criteria upon which a diagnosis could be based; this list can be found in their *Diagnostic and Statistical Manual of Mental Disorders* (DSM). Although autism is considered a neurological disorder, rather than psychiatric, the DSM-IV criteria for autism is generally the accepted standard for diagnosis. When Derek was recently qualifying for state and federal assistance, a physician had to complete a checklist of the DSM criteria for approval.

When I suspected Derek was autistic, I struggled to find anyone willing to formally diagnosis him until I found his then-pediatrician. Before the DSM criteria for autism was written, it remained a nebulous label. Now, I believe that autism is being overdiagnosed, using the ASD blanket, which is causing confusion in the areas of intervention and placement. The diagnostic criteria keep changing, and the categories included in the diagnosis of ASDs have increased. The effect is that autism appears to be increasingly prevalent.

I can understand wanting to have an easy target to aim the

frustration and grief that comes with the diagnosis of autism, but I would rather spend our time, energy, and funds on solid research that may truly make headway in the understanding of this confounding disorder. I no longer have any patience for the anecdotal coincidences or "cures" that have come and gone over the years. (My favorite is bathing in pineapple juice.) The best, most comprehensive article I've read on this issue is "Fear Not" by Dr. Steven Novella (found at the Web address www.theness.com/articles.asp?id=74). In it, Dr. Novella, a professor of neurology at Yale University School of Medicine, refutes a lot of nonsense related to autism, especially about the supposed dangers of immunizations. Dr. Novella's writing is a breath of fresh air, and I highly recommend this article, as well as his others. He also has a blog at www.theness.com/neurologicablog.

When an epidemiologist recently told me that a leading cause of death of those with autism is peritonitis (an intra-abdominal infection) from an undiagnosed ruptured appendix, I found it sad, yet interesting. It is likely that limited communication and a seemingly unresponsive reaction to pain are contributing factors to this disturbing statistic. About a year ago, Derek was walking across our deck when his leg broke through one of the boards and an exposed nail gouged a ten-inch cut on the front of his thigh. It had to have been incredibly painful, but Derek didn't make a sound. He quietly came to me with a look on his face that seemed more bewildered than pained. (Because of the lack of reaction to pain, some mistakenly believe that those with autism have unusually high pain thresholds. Several verbal individuals with autism have told me that it is, rather, an inability to express pain, whether physical or emotional.) Blood streamed down his leg and pooled around his foot. He was more upset about the mess he was making than any pain he felt. He usually does not tolerate small bandages for minor cuts, but he left the large dressing alone while the wound healed, seeming to understand that it was serving an important purpose.

Stages of Grief

When a child is given the devastating diagnosis of autism, parents commonly react with anger. Dr. Elisabeth Kubler-Ross, an authority in the field of death, dying, and transition, was the first to identify the five stages of grief—a cycle that people experience when confronted with death, terminal illness, or a life-changing event. These stages are denial, anger, bargaining, depression, and acceptance. I believe parents whose children are diagnosed with autism go through these stages just as though their child had died. Almost seventeen years after Derek was diagnosed, my husband is probably still in the anger stage, whereas I accepted the diagnosis long ago.

Sometimes we hear anecdotal reports of those with autism who are supposedly cured or even vastly improved by some unproven treatment. I believe it is cruel to spotlight these stories because they make some parents, who are doing their uttermost, feel like they are falling short. They wonder why their children are still struggling. The last thing they need is a guilt trip on top of the sorrow they are experiencing. Children with autism do still develop and learn and will emerge from their initial withdraw in varying degrees. Many of the changes, large and small, that parents witness are the growth and development of a nurtured child.

Chapter 21

SENSITIVITIES AND SEMANTICS

I had never participated in any message boards or blog sites, but when we were planning to change Derek's medications, I posted an inquiry about side effects experienced by those who were taking the drugs we were considering. I got some useful information and opinions, but I also received a barrage of unbelievable responses. Evidently, autism has not escaped the current climate of political correctness run amok and is now even a prime target. On one site, a fellow mom admonished me, saying that instead of medicating my child's autism, I should happily accept it. She told me that she even proudly displays such slogans as "Neurodiversity Rocks!" "Autie Pride!" and "Embrace Your Autism!" on bumper stickers and lapel buttons. Further, she was offended by the "Solve the Puzzle of Autism" campaign (www.solvethepuzzle.org) because she believed there is nothing about autism to be solved. I could not disagree more. Her children, whom she refers to as "aspies" (those with Asperger's syndrome), are probably high-functioning, contributing members of society.

I will not be displaying any such cheerleading nonsense. I do not embrace Derek's autism; I loathe it, and I would sell my soul for him to be "neurotypical." Though I am proud of my son for the small successes he has in dealing with the daily difficulties of autism, I experience no "autie pride." Autism is not Derek's identity; it is what happened to him.

I must admit that I was completely unaware of this

neurodiversity movement, which aims to have autism accepted as merely an alternative lifestyle, rather than a neurological disorder. I was dismayed—and a bit amused—by some of the peculiar proclamations people made on various Web sites that were recommended to me. My curiosity was piqued, however, so I looked further into this surreal movement. I found that there are those who bristle at "the most offensive word for autism: disorder." The term *condition* is preferred. Apparently some also take offense at the term *normal*; I suppose this is because a disorder implies abnormality, whereas a condition is merely a state of being. Autism *is* an abnormal disorder that caused my son's *disability*, and no one can be sorrier about that than me.

There seems to be two subgroups to this movement: those who are out to "cure" autism at all costs, and those who do not think that autism is something that should be cured. Some believe that by curing autism, they would destroy the personality or "essence" of the child. There are those who believe that "autism is merely a different way of experiencing the world." A "different way" that requires Derek having to take at least three different daily medications to keep him out of jail or a psych ward? I don't believe that those who are neurodivergent should be celebrated, but they should, of course, be respected and supported. I see this as just another movement to normalize the abnormal, using the same strategies as NAMBLA (North American Man/Boy Love Association), which means to impel the normalcy of pedophilia.

I swear that I even came across a posting espousing the position that self-injurious behaviors of those with autism are actually "freedom of expression." Thus, parents who put helmets on their children to keep them from injuring themselves by continual head banging or eye gouging, or parents who restrain their children in any way are impeding on the kids' rights as individuals.

While surfing these previously uncharted waters, I also learned of another organization, The Autism Acceptance Project (TAAP). A leader in the neurodiversity movement, this group's mission statement includes "We as autistic people and friends and family of autistic individuals, do not see autism as a tragic epidemic. We view autism as a part of life—with both challenges and abilities that deserve to be accommodated." TAAP's goal is to bring a positive view of autism to the public. Some consider the word *autistic* to be insensitive (I am not one of them). It is used twice, antithetically, in the mission statement of a group advocating for those with autism. I admit that I'm confused, but I'm assuming that those who embrace their autism refer to themselves as "autistic" or even collectively as "autistics," and those who aren't quite to the point of "autie pride" still want to be referred to as "individuals with autism." This is all silly to me, as I think one's intentions and actions are more important than their semantics.

On a positive note, there is a worldwide online community of those with autism who are computer literate. I think it is wonderful that we have this ability to network, relate, and communicate with others who experience the same struggles, issues, and successes in an often very lonely world. The same identity safeguards for any online and often anonymous communication should be in place and supervised when appropriate.

On the Flip Side

Still, on the complete opposite side of the coin, words do matter. I know that Whitney or Dylan could never utter the word "retard" (the "R word") because of the way they were raised, even if Derek was not their brother. Our family prefers "developmentally delayed." Derek is officially labeled as "autistic," but many with this diagnosis are also considered mentally retarded because of their low IQ scores. (It is very difficult to accurately test individuals with autism, especially those who are nonverbal.)

With all of the stifling political correctness, I am dumbfounded by the ugly resurgence of the "R word." I hear it all of the time at Derek's high school. When this happens, the young offenders are told how deeply their cruel, flippant comment can hurt their fellow classmates. My sensitivity is not for Derek, as he does not care in the least how anyone refers to him; it is for those students who very well understand the ugly slur.

My daughter, who is in a progressive college in California, tells me that she hears the R word on campus all the time. These same students wouldn't dream of commenting on the ethnic differences among them. Increased awareness is the only way I know to counter this unfortunate trend, and I hope this mention will help in some small way.

When I was in elementary school, I was student volunteer who pushed students in wheelchairs to lunch and art class. During this time, I presented my school and parents with a serious dilemma when I punched a kid who was imitating an ambulant student with cerebral palsy in our group. I was not present at the meeting to discuss appropriate consequences, but I do remember that the little creep got nothing in the way of punishment—except a fat lip from me—and I almost got detention instead of a citation. That said, my mom and dad did share that they were proud of me.

I grew up with my mom's best friend, Marion, and her four kids; we were like one big family. Marion's son Dougie, who was about six years older than me, was developmentally delayed. He probably functioned at a five-year-old level in his adulthood, but he could put together difficult jigsaw puzzles in record time. He was a sweet kid who grew into a fairly independent adult. He always held down a job and was able to successfully use the Miami transit system, which overwhelms me. Marion died a few years ago, but the last time I spoke with her, she marveled at how ironic it was that she was actually dependent on him at that point in her life. I will always think kindly of this friendly, funny, warm, and accepting woman, who did the very best for her son as a single mom, during some pretty tough times. I like to think that Derek may now be benefiting from some of the lessons I learned from her.

Chapter 22

INTERVENTIONS

I have never been one to suffer fools gladly, and I don't want to waste any more time or resources on new age nonsense and conspiracy theories. I believe that finding real therapies that will improve the lives of our children is just too important. Indigo moms, whose little crystals are crazed with yeastiness, jonesing for gliadomorphins, and those who believe that government officials are in secret societies with "Big Pharm" execs, who meet when the moon is full to plot the poisoning of our children, while the CDC covers it up, probably won't absorb much of this chapter. I do not believe in magic, and I spend no energy being angry at dubious causal targets. I have found that persistence, advocacy, appropriate medications, a sense of humor, and love is what has helped my family the most. Different interventions work for different kids at different times. Regardless of the diagnosis or placement on a spectrum, each child will have unique problems and needs; those are what we need to address. Treatments and interventions are not for the autism, which is not curable, but rather for the symptoms and behaviors that are manifestations of autism. Each child is an individual, regardless of his or her autism.

Reputable studies are currently being done to examine a possible association between autism and immune system abnormalities. Derek doesn't exhibit any immunity problems; he has the constitution of a buffalo, and I can count the number of times he has been ill on one hand. Let's see: Montezuma's revenge in Mexico, an overindulgence of begonias in 1991, a spider bite on his finger, and a mild case of chicken pox when he was five.

Many books I have read about autism were written by parents of young children and parents full of hope and optimism. I believe that to publish only books about miracles and promises of cures is a terrible disservice to other parents of autistic children, who are made to feel guilty for being unable to produce the same improvements in their children. I don't believe there is a cure, but I do believe that the quality of life for those born with autism can be greatly improved with early intervention and hard work. I still have hope and expectations for my son, but I focus more on strategies than treatment. I feel somewhat foolish for having tried some of the remedies that have been touted or recommended over the years that I knew were anecdotal and unfounded. But none of them were harmful or particularly costly; at least I have no regrets about what might have worked, if I had only tried. Most of the remedies, at best, rendered nothing more than expensive urine.

I am a realist and find satisfaction in doing what is truly helpful for Derek. How do I view those who claim that an autistic child is cured suddenly and becomes miraculously "normal"? Perhaps the child had a lessening of symptoms or learned better behaviors or was misdiagnosed to begin with. I don't know of one person who was truly cured of his or her autism. A lot of help and good information is out there, but there is also sensationalism, false hopes, and fear mongering. Strategies just work better than quackery. I tend to be cynical by nature and skeptical from experience, so I will give my candid and honest opinion of interventions that I am familiar with.

The first thing a parent with an autistic—and especially a nonverbal—child should do is put an augmentative communication system in place. When the child has a functional way to express himself, frustration is mitigated and undesired behaviors are greatly reduced. One can easily do this at very little cost. I would suggest starting out with clear photographs of foods or items the child highly desires, as motivation is key. Have the child sit at his desk while the teacher or facilitator sits on the opposite side of the desk. In front of the child, place the desired item next to the corresponding picture of it. Until the exchanges become successful, have another person stand behind the child and offer hand-over-hand assistance. The second adult takes the child's hand, helping him pick up the picture to hand it to the sitting adult. The sitting adult then says, "Oh, you want a Skittle. Here you are," and gives the child the candy. Eventually, the child may be able to communicate by constructing picture or icon "sentences." A good book that further explains this method, along with some others, is *A Picture's Worth: PECS and Other Visual Communication Strategies in Autism* by Andy Bondy and Lori Frost.

Another useful instructional and informative book is *A Treasure Chest of Behavioral Strategies for Individuals with Autism* by Beth Fouse and Maria Wheeler. It offers several strategies and interventions that parents or teachers can use to control aberrant behaviors or replace them with desired ones. ABA (Applied Behavior Analysis; see Glossary), boiled down, are the principles that I use most: anticipate and diffuse, redirect, reward the positive, and ignore the negative.

I love to watch the television show *Supernanny* because it features the queen of behavior modification; however, even her most challenging charge is a piece of cake compared to Derek. The success of the *Dog Whisperer* is from his expert use of firm yet gentle behavioral training. Implementing behavioral tactics into your lives offers boundaries, structure, and predictability that your child will find reassuring. There is no magic to behavior therapy, and parents don't have to mortgage their house to afford it. I know of some autism treatment programs in California that are costing between $30,000 and $150,000! It is just hard work that you can do yourself after some initial instruction. Consistency and persistence are the keys to success.

Parent should share any helpful books or information they find with the child's teacher. It is important that both fronts are on the same page so that the home and school environments reinforce each other. It is also important that the child's teacher is familiar with structured teaching, an excellent example of which is the TEACCH model (www.teacch.com). This is an internationally recognized treatment and support modality for individuals with autism that was founded by Gary Mesibov, among others. Using the same communication system at home and at school is important as well. I suggest avoiding any behavior therapist—or anyone, for that matter—who uses any type of aversive interventions. The most common one of these, which I still see, is spraying the child in the face with various liquids. This method is hardly conducive to developing a rapport with the child, which is critical to successful learning.

There are also therapies or treatments that I wouldn't waste one penny on (or space here to explain them). These include:

- FC (facilitated communication)
- Vitamin/mineral therapy (B6, magnesium, inositol)
- DMG (dimethylglycine)
- AIT (auditory integration training)
- Gluten or casein restriction
- NAET (Namburdripad's Allergy Elimination Technique)

- BIT (Brain Integration Therapy)
- Infrared saunas
- Gold ingestion of any kind.

Also, stay away from chelation therapy (used to remove heavy metals from the body) of any kind—heavy metals have not been shown to contribute to autism. (Derek tested negative for heavy metals and has never had a filling.) Mercury does not cause autism—several recent studies show that the rates of autism continued to rise, years after mercury was removed from vaccines. I have lost patience with all the nonsense that unsuspecting parents have to wade through as they try to find appropriate treatment.

Several years ago, anecdotal reports began surfacing about autistic children who were given a single dose of intravenous secretin during an endoscopy for conditions unrelated to autism. Subsequently, they experienced a marked improvement in speech and eye contact. We experienced no such result. In addition, follow-up clinical trials produced no evidence for any improvement in symptoms associated with autism.

Irlen (tinted) lenses filter out various frequencies of the light spectrum to help those with visual sensitivities. Those with autism or other neurologic disorders can experience symptoms of these problems, such as glare, double vision, or blurring when reading. Derek isn't able to tell me if the colored lenses did anything for him, but he showed no interest in them. I remember reading that Donna Williams, author of *Nobody, Nowhere*, said the lenses helped her with visual and perceptual distortions. Irlen lenses are generally considered a controversial therapy, as their effectiveness has not been empirically proven. I see no harm in trying them if your child is able to express that they make a difference for him or her. I still occasionally see samples that people can try at product booths set up at conventions and conferences.

Derek doesn't have leaky gut syndrome (an intestinal dysfunction) or any other gastrointestinal (GI) disorders. Individuals with autism do seem to experience gastrointestinal symptoms, but the rate is probably no higher than the general population. GI problems and autism are not mutually exclusive, but I don't believe they are necessarily related. Persistent vomiting, diarrhea, or anorexia warrants a visit to a board-certified gastroenterologist. Lab reports from mail-in poop samples should not be taken seriously.

Research is currently underway to study the possible association between the GI tract and the brain, with the vagus nerve serving as the link. The vagus nerve is the longest cranial nerve, extending from the brain through the neck and chest into the abdomen. It is involved in regulating satiety and overriding pain pathways, which might help explain why Derek occasionally gulps water to the point of vomiting. He seems to experience no discomfort even when his abdomen becomes greatly distended. He might be getting some kind of positive feedback in his brain from what his gut is sensing. I will be very interested in the results of these studies.

Genuine Therapy or Snake Oil?

I think the perceived increased incidence of autism has caused a rise in novel therapies, as companies and individuals hope to cash in on the "trend." Some therapies are just common-sense practices that have been given slick packaging, heavy marketing, and exorbitant price tags; some are just pure snake oil. Here are a few of the more popular therapies:

- Some reports indicate that children experience

temporary increases in spatial reasoning after listening to Mozart—this has become known as the Mozart effect. It certainly won't hurt your child to listen to classical music—Derek doesn't seem to mind it—but I question whether it's actually a beneficial "treatment."

- Craniosacral therapy is another novel approach. It involves using gentle touch to help balance the cerebrospinal fluid and the membranes that surround the spine and brain. It purports to improve central nervous system function and dissolve the effects of stress. I think it's nonsense, but Dr. Stephen Barrett humorously skewers its claims far better than I could ever hope to on his Quackwatch Web site: www.quackwatch.org/01QuackeryRelatedTopics/cranial.html.

- Sensory integration therapy (SIT) is designed for those with sensory integrative dysfunction (those who have trouble processing information received through the senses), which many individuals with autism experience. The purpose of SIT is to improve the ability to use incoming sensory information (whether through touch, movement, sights, sounds, tastes, or smells) and increase the individual's tolerance of the sensory information that is troubling. I have not been impressed with the reported results of the therapy, although it includes activities that some children may find calming, such as spinning, rocking, skin brushing, and massage. Many insurance companies do not cover SIT, however, and most neurologists do not recognize sensory integrative dysfunction as a diagnosis. An excellent article on this topic appears on www.quackwatch.org: "Why 'Sensory Integration Disorder' Is a Dubious Diagnosis" by Dr. Peter L. Heilbroner.

Still, SIT may be beneficial for some. Although Derek

was never a "spinner" or "twirler," he has always loved to swing and jump on a trampoline. These activities calm him and help him release his anxiety. Fast walking also helps when a swing or trampoline is not available. Another gross motor activity that we use to expend excess energy is stomping aluminum cans from the recycling bins. Derek also enjoys deep pressure massage but is not a good candidate for SIT massage because he doesn't like the weighted vests or blankets that SIT often uses.

- Hyperbaric oxygen therapy (HBOT), used to treat nitrogen narcosis (the bends), is currently touted as a treatment for myriad diseases and conditions, one of which is autism. Using HBOT—which includes sitting in an enclosed (hyperbaric) chamber as a method of administering pure oxygen—to treat autism is based on the faulty premise that autism was caused by hypoxia (lack of oxygen supply to the brain) before or during birth. This claim has not been proven, and reports of improvement using HBOT are only anecdotal. Derek would need general anesthesia in order to get him to spend an hour in the claustrophobic, coffin-shaped chamber, and that would probably defeat the purpose. He also would not tolerate the hooded hyperbaric treatment, which uses a "hood" (like a giant fish bowl worn over the head) as the means to administer oxygen, which can cause uncomfortable ear pressure.

I'm no apologist for drug companies, but I thank God for those companies that manufacture the drugs that allow me to control my son well enough to keep him with us. Some parents, however, seem to blame drug companies for their children's autism, as if they are uncaring entities, bent on ruining the lives of children. I don't see it that way; sometimes bad things happen, and no one is at fault. Much of the abnormal brain development that involves altered neural circuitry—the part of the brain that affects the nervous system, and which is a characteristic of those who develop autism—has been proven to happen in the early stages of pregnancy, not as a result of vaccines or pharmaceutical therapies. Again, *The Neurobiology of Autism* by Margaret Bauman and Thomas Kemper is the best source I know for learning about the legitimate research and the results so far.

We tried various things with Derek, and not everything worked for us, although it's possible that those that didn't work might work for another child. I would just caution you to be aware of the people and organizations who would take advantage of desperate parents. If someone suggests something that seems potentially hazardous, unreasonably expensive, or illogical, *stop*. Do your research and consult with licensed professionals—remember that most medical professionals chose their field because they want to help people.

Commonly Used Drugs

Seeing a physician or other licensed professional who is familiar with medications and has experience using them can be helpful in addressing the behaviors that often accompany autism. For example, we are now working with a nurse practitioner from our state's department of disabilities, who has many clients on various combinations of medications to treat a variety of symptoms. She recommended a new drug regimen for Derek that has been successful.

Some of the most common drugs currently being used to treat symptoms of autism, such as agitation and aggression, are the newer atypical antipsychotics: risperadone (Risperdal), olanzapine (Zyprexa), ziprasidone (Geodon), and aripiprazone (Abilify).

Derek was on risperadone for about six years and experienced a marked reduction in agitation and aggressive behaviors and had no side effects on low doses. When increased doses became necessary, however, he experienced significant weight gain. Extrapyramidal side effects—those related to movement and coordination—such as tardive dyskinesia (involuntary movements of the tongue, lips, face, trunk, and extremities) may occur with dosages exceeding 5 mg per day.) When Derek began to exhibit manic rages—he was later diagnosed as bipolar—he was given aripiprazone (Abilify) and gabapentin (Neurontin) instead of risperadone and has thus far responded well.

Derek also takes 25–50 mg of trazadone at bedtime to help him sleep through the night. This is an older antidepressant that may produce the side effect of sedation. This has worked well for us; before we used it, Derek would wake during the night, almost every night.

When Derek was younger, we tried selective serotonin reuptake inhibitors (SSRI) to treat his aggression but didn't notice any changes, positive or negative. There is, however, reported success with this class of drugs, which includes paroxatine (Paxil), sertraline (Zoloft), and fluoxatine (Prozac).

Another drug that is given to treat anxiety, aggression, and self-injurious behaviors is clonidine. This is an alpha-adrenergic blocker that is usually prescribed for high blood pressure. Possible side effects are sedation, low blood pressure, and dangerous rebound hypertension if the patient misses a dose. Reports show that clonidine does seem to work in improving social behavior, but it is usually given only after SSRIs are found to be unsuccessful after a trial period. For those with symptoms of attention deficit disorder and hyperactivity, central nervous system stimulants, such as dexmethylphenidate (Focalin) or methylphenidate (Ritalin), may be of use.

For emotional instability and mood swings, some anticonvulsant medications have a mood-stabilizing effect. Two of these medications are gabapentin (Neurontin) and lamotrigine (Lamictal).

Lamictal is reportedly more effective in this regard but has a serious side effect: potentially life-threatening and disfiguring skin rashes, including Stevens-Johnson syndrome, a rare and serious disorder that causes the top layer of skin to die and slough off. Careful titration—a process that gradually adjusts the dose of a medication until the desired effect is achieved—helps to mitigate the danger of this side effect, but it's still a little too scary for me.

Chapter 23

COMORBIDITY

Last summer, when Derek was eighteen, we experienced our most difficult period. Derek became increasingly anxious and aggressive and exhibited wild mood swings. When he wasn't hiding in his darkened room, he would constantly pace and stomp around while growling and making high-pitched whining sounds.

On a day when Rex was at work and Dylan had spent the night with a friend, I went down to Derek's room to wake him up. It was a typical summer day, free from the stress of school, and yet he had that wide-eyed, agitated countenance that we were seeing more and more. I knew I had better be on guard, so I gave him his medications right away. He dashed up the stairs and frantically began signing "coffee." I told him to sit down, and I would make him some. I knew that he was barely able to contain himself, so I tried to reassure him while the decaf coffee brewed. He held it together for the first batch and then gluttonously chugged the portion I gave him. He then immediately demanded more. I told him that I would make more when he calmed down and behaved, to which he responded by screaming and jumping up and down. I told him to go to his room to calm down. He was the most agitated I had ever seen him, so I locked his bedroom door. All sorts of banging sounded from his room, escalating to the point where the whole house was shaking. The cats sought shelter, and I yelled at Derek to stop.

Derek then started kicking his bedroom door. I should have

just ignored him, but he was clearly doing serious damage. When I went down the stairs again, the door to his room exploded, along with the entire frame. He emerged through the wreckage and bolted toward me. I tripped as I ran up the stairs, and he ran right over me. I regained my footing and tried to grab him, but he head-butted me to get away. He made his way out the front door and continued to jump up and down, screaming like a banshee for about twenty minutes. The two methods that had previously worked to control Derek when he blew—my ability to "intimidate," and the safe room that was his retreat—suddenly ceased to be. I felt completely impotent and worried that I wasn't going to be able to handle him any longer. I knew Rex wasn't going to be able to get home anytime soon, so I called the agencies that are now in place since he is considered an adult (DSHS, DDD, and SSI).

I received the ubiquitous, annoying voice mails instructing me to push different numbers for services I didn't need. I left the following message: "My son is an eighteen-year-old who is autistic. He is twice my size and is becoming increasingly violent. He just came through a solid wood door and over me. I don't think I can control him anymore. He seems now to realize his strength, and his aggressiveness is escalating with each episode. I'm afraid that the day I've been dreading but expecting has come, and I really don't know what to do." I must have gotten someone's attention, because my call was returned within minutes. By then Derek's medications had begun to work, and he had calmed down somewhat. I no longer needed emergency assistance, but I was impressed to find out that the next day, Derek's caseworker would be coming for an intervention, along with a nurse practitioner, who would discuss medication options. A behavior specialist also would be consulted.

Unfortunately, their response to Derek's behavior of the day before was exactly what I didn't want to hear. They gave me a group-home placement, which was on the other side of the state and which was the only option until he turned twenty-one. If I was able to drive him across the state, I wouldn't have been on the phone asking for immediate help. Their other suggestion was to call the police the next time he became violent. This was also not an option for me.

I surprised myself when I said, "We need to slow down; I'm not ready yet. I just cannot consider a group-home placement at this point." Did that mean I would consider it at *some* point, when I had always insisted I never would?

I knew a physically dependent young man who contracted a venereal disease after he was placed in a group home as an adult. He died within a year of his placement—that did it for me. Derek is big now and can be a little scary, but he is still basically a naïve four-year-old. Before that episode, I know I would have been indignant at the mere mention of a group home for my son. I was disgusted at myself for even considering it for a moment. And still, I am faced with the reality that a group home is just where he will end up at some point if we cannot figure out an alternative.

When I was able to reach my husband, clearer heads prevailed, and he suggested changing the medication dosages before taking any drastic measures. This is exactly what the nurse practitioner suggested when she came to our home.

The increased medication regimen worked for about two weeks, and then Derek had another major blowup when Rex and Dylan were home. We kept his door opened so he wouldn't break it down again before we could better reinforce it. He kept signing for "pop," jumping and screaming, and then he bit Rex on the shoulder. A week after that Derek again became agitated, but we were able to give him more medication and placate him before his agitation was full-blown. These episodes lasted about thirty minutes and seemed to be happening more frequently, which we found concerning. We were trying to adjust his meds so he didn't experience the wild mood swings and emotional instability, but we obviously weren't quite successful. To make matters more difficult, most of the time Derek held things together and was his affable self, but we needed to address and prevent the aggressive episodes as much as possible. I think I was suffering from "pre"-traumatic stress syndrome. I would wake up in the morning wondering if I was going to have to do battle with a crazed adult male who used to be my cute little boy. I was reluctant to take him out in the community as I always had, for fear of his blowing up in public and wreaking havoc. Tragically for Derek, his world had gotten a whole lot smaller.

I hope to gain some insight into this situation by having the school psychologist complete a functional behavior analysis (FBA). Behavioral psychologists study what happens before, during, and after undesirable behaviors occur. They question what purpose or function the behavior serves. They will try to determine whether we are somehow rewarding Derek with attention or caving in to his demands to calm him down. I used to be able to ignore him when he had a "tantrum," but now that he's upped the ante with his recent escalation in behaviors, I'm not sure what to do when he is being really destructive and aggressive. I hope the FBA will afford us some useful suggestions or a plan to de-escalate the situation and prevent unacceptable behaviors.

If his behaviors have gotten this bad at home where he is happiest, I dread taking him to school, his least favorite place. Before school starts, I will stock up his schoolroom with favorite things like a mini-trampoline in the hope that will help him see school as a place he enjoys, rather than a place he dreads. I'm also going to talk to his teacher about coming up with some jobs he can perform at school, such as shredding paper, picking up trash, or sorting recyclables. I know Derek would prefer these chores to tedious and repetitive tasks like those in the vocational skills boxes, which were a main source of his anxiety last year. The transition period at high school is for job training anyway, making these activities not only appropriate but preferable.

The high school teacher next year is a gentle, unflappable professional who is perfect for Derek and his stressed-out mom. I know he will do what he can to accommodate our needs. I have warned everyone of the increased potential for disaster, and we have had meetings to prepare for the likelihood of major meltdowns. His teacher is updating Derek's crisis response plan. As Derek struggles to adjust to high school, I will continue to repeat my current mantra of "three more years." I'm sure Derek's school district will be doing the same.

A New Diagnosis

I guess autism just was not interesting enough for me. It seems the reason for Derek's recent regression, agitation, wild mood swings, and escalating aggression is because he is also bipolar. (Evidently, there is about a 30 percent comorbidity of the two disorders.) My first reaction was, "You have got to be kidding me!" I allowed myself a day of "this seriously sucks," but then I thought of his many classmates with debilitating and heartbreaking diseases. Also, Derek doesn't have epilepsy, another common comorbid diagnosis of autism, also at a rate of about 30 percent. I'm glad I wasn't given the choice between bipolar and epilepsy, as both can be quite frightening. After my one-day pity party, I hit the books and researched the various treatments for bipolar disorder.

Derek's autism has always had elements of anxiety, OCD (obsessive compulsive disorder), and emotional instability. We are not sure if they are part of autism or are layered over it. I'm leaning toward the former and believe that his recent exacerbation of symptoms may not even be a distinct diagnosis. As we all have learned, it really doesn't matter what you call something (or someone); it is the individual's issues and behaviors that must be dealt with regardless of the labels.

Bipolar disorder (sometimes referred to as manic depression) is hard enough to manage with someone who is able to communicate what he or she is feeling. Getting the right medication at the right level for a particular individual is tricky business. I did, however, find some relief in learning that there is somewhat of an overlap of medications prescribed for some of the symptoms of autism and manic depression. Thus, we would not need a completely new drug regimen, when our current one was becoming tenuous at best. Treatment for this new condition is still a work in progress, but we have seen a lot of improvement in a short amount of time, without making drastic changes to the medications. We have elected to gradually change from Risperdal to Abilify. In addition, we've added Neurontin (usually given as an anti-seizure medication) with impressive results. Derek seems to be back to his happy self with only one exception so far. I haven't breathed a sigh of relief yet, but with each good day we have I become more satisfied that we're on the right track.

Chapter 24

DEREK'S FUTURE

I'm not sure what the future will bring for Derek. I really don't like to think about it but know that I have to plan for it. I do know that I don't want Whitney or Dylan to feel responsible for their brother. Derek has already impacted their lives, in good ways as well as bad, but their futures need to be their own. Because of the decent human beings they've become, I know that if anything happened to Rex or me, they would check in on Derek to make sure he was well cared for and reasonably happy.

Rex's side of the family has seen a lot of longevity. His grandfather is healthy and still active in his nineties. I have visions of Rex and Derek, years from now, touring the country in a motor home and stopping to eat at every Denny's along the way. If I live that long, I'll stay home with the animals and keep an album of the postcards they send me from their adventures.

When going through my files of articles recently, I came across one by Karl Taro Greenfeld in *Time* magazine (May 6, 2002). He is the brother in the *Noah* book series (see Book Recommendations) written by his father, Josh Greenfeld. In it, he said that Noah had been institutionalized since he was eighteen. I was saddened to learn this, as it made me wonder anew whether Derek would share Noah's fate at some point. I remember so relating to *A Child Called Noah* when Derek was little. That book gave me permission to own the wide-ranging emotions that come in response to having a severely autistic child.

I recently reread the series, which are really Josh Greenfeld's journals since the birth of his sons. His books are raw and real. If it is miraculous cures or false hopes you want, look elsewhere. If you want to know what it is really like to raise an autistic child, I recommend reading the entire series.

The Future Now

With medication, Derek is still manageable as he enters adulthood, but he has challenged and disobeyed me. I'm still able to bluff him into submission, but I'm afraid that one day soon, he'll realize how easy it would be for him to overpower me. When that happens, it will be "game over." I don't know what we'll do, if or when that happens. I hope it won't be an issue any longer, as his new meds seem to be working well, and Derek is his old self again. Now, I cannot think about an adult placement, as the Greenfelds had to do. We'll cross that bridge when or if we get to it. Derek can be aggressive when he is anxious, but more often, he is a sweet, funny, and childlike being who I would protect with my life. That he wouldn't be able to communicate that he was being mistreated causes me so much anxiety that I literally don't let him out of my sight. To totally turn him over to strangers in a strange place would be way too much for this overprotective, control-freak mommy to endure.

I am fairly sure that in next few years, we will experience some growing pains, but with the success of Derek's new medication regimen, I have a renewed faith. During this transition period, Derek will be challenged to learn new job skills in new settings with new people, while still attending the high school that he barely tolerates. I have tried as his aide to get him used to new settings and new routines, and there does seem to be a reason for hope. He recently had one of his best weeks since being at the high school. He is completing all of his "jobs" at school and is even lasting a full day. No one expected such a smooth passage to this stage of increased independence, and I could not be more pleased for him.

As for Me

I haven't had therapy yet, as I'm of the opinion that being sad about a sad situation is a normal reaction. I don't think we are supposed to be happy all of the time. On especially bad days, red wine helps to dull the intensity of emotions. My favorite cat, Ms. Lynxy, is my purring, furry ball of Prozac; she can always make me smile. I have also been able to convince my husband that the white Zappos.com shoe boxes that occasionally show up on our porch are a lot cheaper than a shrink.

Recently, I stood alone in the wee hours of the night, observing a lunar eclipse and savoring the rare solitude and tranquility. And I reflected back over the many banal years that have been interspersed with frenetic episodes, all of which comprise our lives. As the earth cast its shadow over its planetary partner, the moon gradually disappeared from the black night sky. A large white owl silently soared overhead, amid the darting bats. My life is far from perfect, I realized, but it is rich. I closed my eyes and basked in the warmth of the summer night—and in the warmth generated from within and fueled by the love of family. I felt recharged for the inevitable bumps to come. When I opened my eyes, the moon had returned to its rightful position.

My universe no longer has any room for resentment or

bitterness—only the occasional "what if" that sneaks in, but that is less and less frequent.

My hope for Derek is that he is able to find meaningfulness and peace in his confounding world and that he knows how much he is loved. I am not sanguine about his future, but I face it with existential resignation.

Life is not about waiting for the storm to pass;
It is about learning to dance in the rain.
(Author unknown)

"Hope" is the thing with feathers—
That perches in the soul—
And sings the tune without the words—
And never stops—at all.
(Emily Dickinson, 1861)

You must be willing to give up the life you planned;
So you can accept the life that is waiting.
(Joseph Campbell)

Book Recommendations

Bauman, Margaret MD and Thomas Kemper, MD. *The Neurobiology of Autism.*

Bondy, Andy PhD. *A Picture's Worth: PECS and Other Visual Communication Strategies in Autism*

Cohen, Shirley. Targeting Autism.

Fouse, Beth PhD and Maria Wheeler, M.Ed. A Treasure Chest of Behavioral Strategies for Individuals with Autism.

Grandin, Temple. *Emergence.*

Grandin, Temple. *Thinking in Pictures.*

Greenfeld, Josh. A Child Called Noah.

Greenfeld, Josh. *A Client Called Noah.*

Greenfeld, Josh. *A Place for Noah.*

Hodgdon, Linda M.Ed. *Solving Behavior Problems in Autism.*

Hodgdon, Linda M.Ed. Visual Strategies for Improving Communication.

Koegel, Robert and Lynn Koegel. *Pivotal Response Treatments for Autism: Communication, Social, and Academic Development.*

Koegel, Robert and Lynn Koegel. Teaching Children with Autism.

Leaf, R. and J. McEachin. A Work in Progress: Behavior Management Strategies and a Curriculum for Intensive Behavioral Treatment of Autism.

Mesibov, Gary, Lynn Adams, and Laura Klinger. *Autism: Understanding the Disorder.*

Mesibov, Gary, Victoria Shea and Eric Schopler. *The TEACCH Approach to Autism Spectrum Disorder.*

Park, Clara Claiborne. The Siege

Powers, Michael PsyD. *Child with Autism: A Parent's Guide*

Schreibman, Laura. Autism.

Senator, Susan. *Making Peace with Autism.*

Siegel, Bryna. The World of the Autistic Child

Watson, Lord, Schaffer, and Schopler. Teaching Spontaneous Communication to Autistic and Developmentally Handicapped Children.

Web Sites

www.autismspeaks.com

This organization has been very successful increasing autism awareness and raising funds for research.

www.cdc.gov/ncbddd/autism

This Centers for Disease Control Web site includes the 2007 report on autism.

www.quackwatch.org

This Web site is "Your Guide to Quackery, Health Fraud, and Intelligent Decisions" and is operated by Dr. Stephen Barrett.

www.ladders.org/autism.php

This is the site for Learning and Developmental Disabilities Evaluation and Rehabilitative Services. The Autism Research Foundation, founded by Drs. Margaret Bauman and Thomas Kemper, is part of this organization.

www.teacch.com

The Treatment and Education of Autistic and Related Communication-Handicapped Children is an excellent educational model that emphasizes structure, the use of schedules, and physical boundaries, all of which are essential in the teaching of children with autism. I've also included books on my recommendations list by the founder of the program, Eric Schopler.

Check out the *Advocate*'s interview of Dr. Schopler at http://teacch.com/schoplerinterview.html.

www.exploringautism.org

This Web site focuses on the latest information on the genetic component of autism but also includes several other topics and links.

www.dougflutiejrfoundation.org

This Web site is in honor of Doug Flutie's son, Doug Jr., who has autism. Its stated goal is to "promote awareness and support families affected by autism spectrum disorders."

http://faculty.washington.edu/dawson

Dr. Geraldine Dawson is a professor of psychology at the University of Washington. She is the author of *Autism: Nature, Diagnosis and Treatment*. In addition to biographical information about Dr. Dawson, this site also includes some very useful links on autism.

www.cesa7.k12.wi.us/sped/autism/structure/str11.htm

This site gives examples of visual schedules that "are a critical component of a structured environment," which is key to successful learning for those with autism.

www.mayinstitute.org

The May Institute was named 2007 National Award Recipient in Applied Behavior Analysis. The institute provides "comprehensive, research-validated services to children and adults with autism."

www.floortime.org

The mission of this foundation is to broaden the use of the DIR/ Floor time model to redefine the potential of children with developmental and communication challenges. The site also offers DVDs and more information about techniques.

www.fda.gov/cber/vaccine/thimerosal.htm

This site offers detailed information in a question/answer format, reassuring the safety of childhood vaccines since discontinuation of the use of thimerosal as a preservative.

www.wrightslaw.com

The mission of this site is "to provide parents, advocates, educators and attorneys with accurate, up-to-date information about special education law and advocacy so they can be effective catalysts." The site offers several links as well as books and DVDs.

http://idea.ed.gov/explore/home

This site is self-described as a "one-stop shop for resources related to IDEA"—the Individuals with Disabilities Education Act, which is a law ensuring services for children with disabilities throughout the nation.

www.supportforfamilies.org/internetguide/index.html

The Internet Resources for Families of Children with Disabilities is a site whose goal is "to bring together a selection of some of the better resources on the Internet, organize them in an accessible manner, and provide brief annotations." This is a great site for families with a newly diagnosed child. It is easy to navigate and includes many valuable links.

www.aboutautism.org

Sign up for a free subscription to the Southwest Autism Research & Resource Center's *Outreach* magazine, which is geared toward those impacted by autism. This site offers direct, no-nonsense information about autism, including genetic explanations.

http://autism.about.com/od/treatmentoptions

This is the most all-encompassing site I have found. It addresses virtually everything about autism and offers varying perspectives on topics considered controversial.

www.autism-society.org

The Autism Society of America publishes the *Advocate* magazine for members. The site includes information on the annual convention on autism.

www.informingfamilies.org

This Web site is broken down into age groups so you can access only the information that is relevant to your situation. This division is helpful in navigating the daunting alphabet soup when your child is diagnosed with a developmental disability.

www.thearc.org

As stated on its site: "The Arc is the world's largest community based organization of and for people with intellectual and developmental disabilities. It provides an array of services and support for families and individuals "

www.arcwa.org

The Arc of Washington State "has been a leader in the development of services and programs for people with developmental disabilities of all ages and providing support to their families."

http://grandin.com/inc/mind.web.browser.html

This is an interesting article by Temple Grandin, titled "My Mind is a Web Browser: How People with Autism Think."

http://rsaffran.tripod.com/schools.html

This site is basically a warning to parents to beware of school programs that claim to use an ABA approach but don't adhere to a standard of practice that would be acceptable to those who devised this program.

www.nichcy.org/pubs/outprint/ts6txt.htm

This publication, "Vocational Assessment: A Guide for Parents and Professionals," pertains to those in high school in transition. It is produced by the National Information Center for Children and Youth with Disabilities.

www.transitioncoalition.org/~tcacs/new/files/voctransassess.pdf

This Web site offers information and support "related to the transition from school to adult life for youth with disabilities." Vocational transition assessment.

http://vocserve.berkeley.edu/Briefs/Brief62.html

This is an article "Vocational Assessment Practices: What Works" by Richard C. Lombard

www.our-kids.org

This is a networking site for families with children with developmental disabilities.

www.ucdmc.ucdavis.edu/mindinstitute

"The MIND Institute is an international, multidisciplinary research organization, committed to excellence, collaboration and hope, striving to understand the causes and develop better treatments and ultimately cures for neurodevelopmental disorders."

www.socialsecurity.gov/disabilityresearch/wi/pass.htm

www.workworld.org/wwwebhelp/impairment_related_work_expenses.htm

www.ssa.gov/ssi/spotlights/spot-work-expenses.htm
These Web sites offer information and direction for obtaining help with work-related expenses, such as job coaches and necessary tools used for employment.

www.panhandleautism.org

The Panhandle Autism Society wishes to enhance the lives of individuals with autism spectrum disorder (ASD) in Idaho's five northern counties.

www.ideapractices.org

The Idea Partnerships are four national projects funded by the U.S. Department of Education's Office of Special Education Program (OSEP) to deliver a common message about the landmark 1997 reauthorization of the Individuals with Disability Act (IDEA).

www.scerts.com/scerts_model_collaborators.htm

The SCERTS Model focuses on enhancing social communication, emotional regulation, and transactional support for children with ASD and related social communication disabilities.

www.augresources.com

This Web site offers augmentative products for purchase, including Visual Foods Photo Software, which has over 3,500 photographs of different foods.

www.superduperinc.com

This publishing company provides a wide variety of educational and testing materials.

www.feat.org
www.featwa.org

Families for Early Autism Treatment. FEAT is a "non-profit organization of parents, family members, and treatment professionals dedicated to providing best outcome education, advocacy and support …"

www.coping.org/intervention/ftpres/index.htm

This site offers a PowerPoint presentation on Stanley Greenspan's model of "floor time," a way of interacting with young children with autism who are particularly hard to reach.

References

The Advocate. 2007 First Edition

1997 Amendments to the Individuals with Disabilities Education Act.

Autism Society of America. "What Is Autism?" *The Advocate* 29, no. 2 (1997): 3.

Barrett, Stephen M.D. "Why Craniosacral Therapy Is Silly."

Bateman, Barbara. (1991) Better IEPs: Doing It the Right Way.

Bauman, M., and T. Kemper. *The Neurobiology of Autism,* 2d ed. Baltimore:
The John Hopkins University Press, 2005.

Bondy, A., and L. Frost. *A Picture's Worth: PECS and Other Visual Communication Strategies in Autism.* Bethesda, Maryland: Woodbine House, 2002.

Centers for Disease Control and Prevention. "2007 Report on Autism." www.cdc.gov/ncbddd/autism.

Claiborne, C. *The Siege: The First Eight Years of an Autistic Child.* Canada: Little, Brown and Company Limited: 1967.

Cohen, S. *Targeting Autism: What We Know, Don't Know, and Can Do to Help Young Children with Autism and Related Disorders.* Berkeley: University of California Press, 1998.

Denes, Shary. "Help Wanted: Adults with Autism Bring Unique Value to the Workplace." Autism Advocate, 1st edition (2007).

DSM IV 299.0

Gorman, Christine. "Do Vaccines Cause Autism?" *Time,* November 18, 2002.

Grandin, T. (2000) "My Mind Is a Web Browser: How People with Autism Think."
Cerebrum 2, no. 1 (winter 2000):14–22. The Charles A. Dana Foundation, New York.

————. *Thinking in Pictures.* New York: Doubleday, 1995.

Grandin, T., and M. M. Scariano. *Emergence: Labeled Autistic.* Novato, California: Arena Press: 1986.

Greenfeld, J. *A Child Called Noah: A Family Journey.* New York: Henry Holt and Company, Inc.: 1970.

————. *A Place for Noah.* New York: Henry Holt and Company, Inc.: 1978.

————. *A Client Called Noah*. New York: Henry Holt and Company, Inc.: 1986.

Koegel, R., and L. Koegel, L. *Teaching Children with Autism: Strategies for Initiating Positive Interactions and Improving Learning Opportunities*. Baltimore: Brookes Publishing Company: 1995.

Leaf, R., and J. McEachin, eds. *A Work in Progress: Behavior Management Strategies and a Curriculum for Intensive Behavioral Treatment of Autism*. New York: DRL Books, L.L.C.: 1999.

Mesibov, G., L. Adams, and L. Klinger. *Autism: Understanding the Disorder*. New York Plemlum Press: 1997.

National Information Center for Children and Youth with Disabilities (NICHCY). "Vocational Assessment: A Guide for Parents and Professionals."

www.nichcy.org/pubs/outprint/ts6txt.htm.

Novella, Steven. "Fear Not." *In Health NW* (Nov–Dec, 2005).

Powers, M. *Children with Autism: A Parent's Guide*. Bethesda, Maryland: The Woodbine House: 1989.

Shakespeare, W. *Macbeth*. In *The Complete Works*. Oxford, New York: The Oxford Press, 1988.

Siegel, B. *The World of the Autistic Child.* New York: The Oxford Press: 1996.

Smith, S., W. Slattery, and T. Knopp. "Beyond the Mandate: Developing Individualized Education Programs That Work for Students with Autism." *Focus on Autistic Behavior* 8, no. 3 (August 1993).

Watson, L., C. Lord, B. Schaffer, and E. Schopler. *Teaching Spontaneous Communication to Autistic and Developmentally Handicapped Children.* New York: Irvington Publishers, 1989.

Appendix

Schedule Samples

These can be typed and laminated so that you can check off each item with a dry erase marker as it is done. This gives children a sense of accomplishment and conveys what is expected of them and how much left they have to do.

School	High School
Michele	puzzles
read	worksheets
work	work boxes
pretzels	video
coffee	LUNCH
swing	walk on track
	play in gym
YMCA	Jobs —water the plants
	recycling
	pick up trash

Guardian Ad Litem Report

Prepared by Richard Perednia, Attorney at Law

Recommendation:

I recommend that Constance Porter be appointed as the full guardian of the person DEREK PORTER. No guardian is being sought for the estate and hence I do not make any recommendations in that regard. Date of appointment is April 3, 2007.

I attest that I am on the Guardian Ad Litem Registry for this County, have conducted approximately 42 Title XI Guardian Ad Litem investigations, and am qualified to serve as Guardian Ad Litem in Guardianship matters.

As required by RCW 11.88.045, I have obtained a written medical/psychological report from the alleged incapacitated person's physician. The report was filed with the Court on April 17, 2007. The examining physician/psychologist was selected by the Guardian Ad Litem. The reason for selecting this individual to prepare the medical psychological report was that she is the treating physician of Derek Porter and is familiar with the Alleged Incapacitated Person and his family.

When I met with Constance Porter I was also able to meet her husband, Rex, and her other son, Dylan. During the course of the interview, I was able to meet alone with the AIP for a few minutes. The alleged Incapacitated Person is nonverbal and cannot speak nor can he read nor write and as a result he was nonresponsive to all of my questions. Although he can communicate to some limited degree using hand signals, he lacks a capacity to speak. He has spent his entire life with his parents in the same residence. His parents stated that they have been married for twenty years and have three children. The oldest daughter, Whitney, is a sophomore in college in California and is not disabled. Derek's younger brother is a fifteen-year-old high school sophomore.

Constance is a registered nurse and had very little knowledge of autism until her psych rotation in training. She said her first child was completely normal, but she could tell that there was something wrong with Derek as early as infancy. At six months old, he made little eye contact. He had some language abilities when he was small, but has lost it. He has little or no understanding of number concepts. He was formally diagnosed as autistic at age two.

He is currently attending high school and is in special education classes. He has exhibited severe behavioral problems at the school setting. Constance is currently serving as his one-on-one aide at school. Rex, Derek's father, is an anesthesiologist. Constance has retired from nursing to devote her time and effort to care for her children, especially Derek. She and her husband work well together in caring for their children. Constance and I also discussed Derek's future, and she indicates that her immediate plan is to take things one day at a time. She indicates that Derek is a physically strong male. She is slighter and older and is concerned about controlling him in the future. He defers to her as his caregiver, but he could over power her if he chose to do so. She said that an adult home may be a possibility at some point, but she will continue to take care of him as long as it is possible. Rex is very much involved with the family. Although Constance has put forth good effort in caring for Derek because he requires such care, Rex is well aware of this and has spent additional time with the other children.

I spoke to Michele, who has been Derek's teacher for almost twelve years. She indicates that it is clear that Derek will need to live with people all of his life and could end up in a group home. He can remain in public schools until he is twenty-one years old. She is working with him on academics and on learning to read at this time in his life. Derek may have some ability to do some kind of job in the future with the right support. She continues to work with him on signing and building on his 120 sight words. She was very complementary of the parenting of his mother, Constance, and states that Derek has benefited greatly from their cooperative efforts. She agreed with my comments that both Rex and Constance have done very well with this very difficult situation.

Derek continues to require twenty-four-hour care and will have to have someone very much involved in his life—whether that this be his parents or in some kind of protective environment such as an adult family home at a later date. I don't feel that he has the capacity to vote, as he cannot read and write.

The guardian will be taking the Spokane County course for nonprofessional guardians. She will prepare annual reports, develop a personal care plan, and is already taking care of Derek very well. She will oversee his education as far as he will go and will plan activities for him in the future.

I certify under penalty of perjury under the laws of the State of Washington that to the best of my knowledge the statements above are true and correct.

Vocational Evaluation / Work Placement Plan

Requested by DVR

Prepared by Gene Christian, MS, CRC

Derek is an eighteen-year-old man who is diagnosed with autism. He is currently a special education student, and it is anticipated that he will continue as a student for three more years.

Derek does not use spoken language but is able to communicate with some sign language and occasional words and gestures. Currently, in addition to attending high school, he receives specific teaching in reading and sight-word recognition with Michele, the special education teacher at his elementary school, in whose classroom he spent eleven years prior before moving to the high school. Derek's mother works as his one-on-one aide in the school setting. Although Ms. Porter is a registered nurse with a specialty in surgery, she works in the aide role because, as she reports, frequent calls from the school requesting her to intervene or come get Derek due to his behavior caused too much disruption in her life for a regular nursing job. As a result, when the school was having difficulty finding and keeping an aide for him, she chose to do so in order to ensure the consistency of his school year. However, her clear preference is that Derek be able to function at school without her presence so Derek can become more independent.

Near the end of Derek's time in Michele's class—in the spring of 2006—he began to show an interest and aptitude for sight-reading. Although Michele had repeatedly tried to work with Derek on reading, he did not show an interest at that time. Since then he has shown dramatic improvement in his ability to sight-read. Currently, he recognizes about 120 words. Michele tutors Derek in word recognition as the first activity of his school day. After that he and his mother go to the high school where Derek is enrolled in a self-contained, special education class. However, educational activities for Derek at the high school appear to be limited to work sample tasks—most of which Derek has mastered. On the day when Derek was observed in tutoring with Michele, he appeared interested in the activity, happy, and very engaged. He would intermittently request snack treats as a reward for his correct responses but managed to spend close to an hour in relatively focused, obviously enjoyable academic interaction with Michele.

However, when Derek was observed later in the day, at the high school, he appeared bored and did not seem to have meaningful activities. First he was observed sitting in a class discussion along with his mother while the teacher had a conversation about sports with members of the class who were verbal and interested in the topic. Derek appeared to neither attend to nor be interested in this activity. Afterwards, Derek stayed to perform work samples with his mother while the other students went elsewhere to complete different activities with the teacher. Derek completes the tasks he is given, but he doesn't seem to enjoy them or find them meaningful. A critical need for Derek appears to be the development of a transitional program that will provide him with a meaningful path to work activities after his high school special education program is completed.

Social Emotional Functioning:

Six core functional-emotional capacities have been defined by two leading clinicians in the field of autism, Stanley Greenspan, MD, and Serena Wieder, PhD. They describe these six core capacities that are the foundation of the ability to relate and communicate as well as the ability to use symbols and ideas for goal-directed purposes. These capacities can be very useful in understanding the strengths and weaknesses that an individual with neurological differences like Derek brings to the vocational rehabilitation process. For the sake of vocational discussion, these six core capacities can be collapsed into three broad traits: (1) the capacity to maintain self-regulation in order to engage with work, problems, and other people (Self-Regulation and Engagement); (2) the capacity to read and understand "Nonverbal Communication" (including apprehending relatively subtle meanings in social situations); and (3) the ability to use language, ideas and for conceptual flexibility in solving workplace problems (Usage of Symbols and Ideas).

An understanding of the strengths and challenges that Derek brings to the vocational rehabilitation process—as well as a potential work placement—may be enhanced by considering his developmental capacities in these critical areas:

The Capacity for Self-Regulation and Engagement: Derek has clear challenges in self-regulation. Although Derek is reported to have a history of violence toward school staff, his mother and teacher both agree that his primary intent when he is upset is to escape. His incidents of physical aggression toward aides and teachers have been the result of attempts to physically block him from leaving an area. Conversations with his mother and teachers about Derek's challenging behavior indicates that he can easily become dysregulated and that, as this happens, his anxiety escalates to the point of genuine fight or flight. As stated, they both agree that Derek's preference is for flight or escape but it is also agreed that, when his physiological system hits this level of upset, he can and will become physically aggressive if anyone gets in his way.

Ms. Porter cites several clear signs that indicate Derek is becoming upset: pacing, high-pitched vocalizations, and an anxious expression on his face. This anxiety is best dissipated through walking—getting away from the situation and burning energy. Another indicator of Derek's anxiety is repeated sign requests for toileting, food, or other forms of escape. Ms. Porter emphasizes that it is important, at these times, to be sure that Derek knows that his requests are understood and, even if they can't be met immediately, to let him know that he is understood by repeating his request back to him and sign "in a minute" to him. Derek's tendency toward dysregulation is often triggered by a lack of predictability with events or interactions. It is important to use both visual and verbal cues to prepare Derek in advance for unanticipated changes in routine.

Strengths: Derek showed the ability to stay focused and happily engaged on a relatively demanding task—work recognition and identification—for up to an hour. He appeared to enjoy the activity, which was characterized by direct interaction from a known and trusted authority figure as well as dense social praise from both his teacher and mother. In addition, this praise was paired with intermittent food rewards. While several minutes is not a substantial period of work, it does suggest that Derek has the potential over time to extend his capacity for work, given the appropriate interpersonal supports and tasks that he enjoys.

Challenges: Derek reportedly has great difficulty staying with any one activity for over a half an hour and will not engage in many nonpreferred activities for even that long—if at all. A consistent trigger for Derek's behavioral outbursts has been having demands made of him. Other triggers can be negative tones of voice or any sense of anger or disapproval in the other person. When Derek begins to be agitated, it is reported that the best way to help him reregulate himself is through walking. For instance, his mother makes it common practice with him to walk the running track outside at school, both when he seems upset and as a preventative measure for helping Derek to keep himself calm. This tendency to become easily dysregulated is probably the central barrier to Derek learning to function in even group-supported employment.

Nonverbal Communication

Strengths: Derek is described as being sensitive to the moods of people around him. However, he has great difficulty with understanding and responding to nonverbal social communication. A primary trigger for Derek's dysregulation is not being able to understand what is expected of him by others. He does not engage in reciprocal interaction with others beyond making simple requests, and these interactions typically consist of no more than three or four circles of communication at a time. It may be that a central reason behind Derek's apparent enjoyment of the daily interactions with Michele on word recognition is that the interchanges are rhythmic, reciprocal, consisting of shared pleasure and ward interpersonal signaling across many circles of communication. The predictability of the interaction makes it accessible for Derek and may be the critical factor that allows him to engage in long chains of shared affect and interaction.

Challenges: As mentioned, Derek, as is typical for people diagnosed with autism, does not understand nor readily respond to preverbal interaction—facial expressions, certain gestures, posture, etc. Also, he craves predictability, reportedly, in terms of both his schedule and social interactions. The possibility of unpredictable demands as well as other forms of unexpected events is, as mentioned, a consistent historical predictor of Derek's problem behavior. Also, confusion regarding interpersonal emotional signals—especially negative emotional signals, whether directed at Derek or not—can often cause him to become agitated.

Usage of Symbols and Ideas

Strengths: Derek is conversant with approximately 120 sight words and is able to sign or match these words to a picture when presented with each of them in a written form. Also, he uses sign language to make requests such as for food, a toilet break, etc. He was observed in my office to repeatedly make the sign for toilet as a way, his mother described, of trying to escape boredom or unfamiliar surroundings.

Challenges: It is not clear how much spoken communication Derek is able to understand. Speech and language evaluation reports from the time that he was in Michele's class suggest that Derek has a much better receptive understanding of the language that he is able to use expressively.

Work-Related Interests: Derek shows few work-related interests. He does enjoy walking and puzzles at school. The former suggests an enjoyment for gross motor activity and the latter suggests some strength in visual-spatial processing. Around his home, Derek puts away the dishes, empties recycling bins, and sometimes engages in yard work such as picking up leaves and transporting them in a wheelbarrow. He also helps with snow shoveling, although it is for only about thirty minutes.

Work-Related Strengths: At present it appears that Derek's work-related strengths are limited. Over time his relative strengths in visual-spatial processing as well as his apparent enjoyment of many gross motor activities could prove to be real strengths in vocational placement. Also, his newly learned skills in sight-word recognition could prove to be a vocational strength over time.

Areas Needing Special Support: Three particular areas in which Derek would need extensive specialized vocational support are prominent:

1) Behavioral-emotional support—Derek's tendency to become easily dysregulated and potentially violent is his most significant barrier to employment of any kind;
2) Work tolerance: At present Derek has difficulty staying with even preferred tasks for over thirty minutes. In order to function in a specialized industry or other form of supported work setting, Derek will need to be able to extend his capacity for staying with one task over time;
3) Communicative support—It is difficult to tease out Derek's problems with dysregulation and challenging behavior from his difficulty communicating with other people and using

them as a source of emotional support. However, because of Derek's apparent difficulty with both expressive and receptive language, it is apparent that he needs special accommodations for communication in order to effectively function in any work setting.

Summary Discussion

Derek is not, at present, a viable candidate for vocational rehabilitation services. Of the three central barriers listed above, the easiest to address is Derek's need for communicative support. His rapidly increasing ability with sight-word recognition, as well as his reported relative strength in language processing, suggest that the easiest barrier to address would be his need for communicative functionally in the workplace, both in terms of understanding directions and responding to work-related problems.

Similarly, Derek's capacity for work tolerance—the ability to persevere with one task across a period of two or more hours at a time—could be slowly increased over time using the behavioral techniques of desensitization, reinforcement, and fading. The desensitization would occur by very gradually increasing the time that Derek is expected to work on any given task each day. These incremental increases would be for periods ranging from one to five minutes and would be accompanied by dense social and tangible (edible) reinforcement. Once Derek was able to continue working without need for breaks or interruption for a targeted period of time, the reinforcement could then be very gradually faded away to a level that would be available in the identified work situation in which he would be expected to perform.

As already emphasized, the greatest barrier to Derek's eventual performance in a work role is his challenging behavior. It needs to be understood that this behavior is not a function of manipulative intent but rather of Derek's difficulty with staying calm and regulated in the presence of demands or expectations—as well as interpersonal stimuli that he finds confusing and threatening.

All of the critical issues should be address over time as part of Derek's school-to-work transition program. Gradual, consistent intervention that addresses work tolerance as well as communication issues could also be tailored to respond to Derek's behavioral difficulties. The first step in such a program would be to replace the one-on-one tutoring and support that is currently provided by his mother with similar support from a different individual who, hopefully, might work with Derek throughout the remainder of his high school career. Replacement of his mother with a nonrelative in the role of educational aide and job coach is desirable for several reasons—not the least of which is his need for increased independence from his mother. Also, in addition to the nonnormalizing nature of having his mother as his job coach and school aide, it will be important, over time, that Derek gradually learn to use other people both to enhance his capacity for self-regulation and to assist him with interpreting and processing difficult interpersonal situations and unpredictable events.

For these reasons, it is recommended that immediate steps be taken to hire and train an aide for Derek. It may be important that both Ms. Porter and Derek have some involvement in the process of choosing this individual. Although Derek is a strong and large individual, the person's capacity for physical control of Derek is not the central issue. The central issue is the aide's potential capacity for understanding Derek's emotional signals of dysregulation and that person's ability to anticipate and calm Derek when he is beginning to experience anxiety.

For these reasons, the replacement of Derek's mother with the new aide should be a gradual process. A new aide should begin by working with Derek while in his mother's presence. By working together with Derek, the aide can develop a rapport while in his mother's presence. After the aide has developed a relationship and learned what dysregulates Derek, how to recognize the signs of his dysregulation, and various strategies for preventing and intervening with Derek's agitation, Ms. Porter can begin to fade her direct involvement at school. Only at this point—after the new aide has become proficient in communicating with Derek and responding to his needs—would his mother begin to fade herself. This would involve her leaving Derek and the aide to work together—at first for brief periods of only a few minutes. Gradually, over the course of week, Derek's day-to-day support at school would be turned over to the new person.

Once this has occurred, consideration should be given to gradually transitioning Derek to a group-supported employment situation—with continuing support from his aide. A specialized industries setting should be identified that has experience working with people with challenges similar to Derek's. Also, this setting should have a work base that consists of work that involves large motor activity. Derek finds this kind of activity both enjoyable and calming. Initially Derek should attend work for only brief periods of time and receive consistent praise—perhaps paired with an edible reward when the work experience is completed each day. Gradually this length of time in a group-supported employment should be extended—the aide continuing to provide full-time support—until Derek is working a period of time each day that is comparable to his peers in that setting.

Additionally, Ms. Porter has provided an article about an

individual with vocational barriers similar to Derek's—autism coupled with serious behavior challenges—who achieved employment in a supported situation with the ongoing assistance of a one-on-one job coach. For this individual, the aide's involvement is considered to be a permanent support and is paid for with a combination of the individual's salary, public funds, and money that the individual saved with the help of a Social Security PASS (Plan to Achieve Self-Support) plan. Consideration should be given to exploring a similar option for Derek when it is appropriate. Despite his communicative/cognitive barriers, it is likely that he would experience both personal satisfaction and a sense of contribution if he were able, over time to develop a successful vocational role.

Considerations and Steps Toward a Viable Vocational Plan

1. At the present time Derek is not a viable candidate for vocational rehabilitation services.
These recommendations are intended for incorporation in his school-to-work transition program, with the possibility that, in three or more years, Derek might be able to successfully function in a supported work role.
2. Derek and his mother should assist with identifying an individual who will replace Ms. Porter as Derek's educational aide for the remainder of his school career.
3. Derek's new aide should work alongside Derek and his mother while learning Derek's personality, needs, and communication style—as well as strategies for preventing and responding to his dysregulation and behavioral excesses.
4. Derek's mother should be gradually faded from being Derek's school aide while the new aide assumes the role that Ms. Porter currently plays in Derek's life.
5. Derek should be gradually introduced to a group-

supported employment situation by beginning to function there for brief (maybe as little as fifteen minutes per day) periods.

6. Derek's one-on-one aide should continue to work with him in the supported setting for the entirety of his school and workday.

7. After Derek is working with the support of a one-on-one aide throughout a typical workdays, decisions should be made as to whether to (a) fade the aide; (b) try to gradually move Derek into a non-group-supported work setting; or (c) continue indefinitely with the full-time aide.

8. The possibility of creating a supported work role—much like was created for the person in the aforementioned article—should be carefully and, perhaps, planned for Derek.

Glossary

ABA—applied behavior analysis is the application of behavior modification in the child's environment using behavior principles to improve the individual's performance and discourage unwanted behaviors. It is an intensive, structured teaching program in which lessons are broken down to their simplest form. Positive reinforcement is used for correct responses while incorrect responses are ignored. ABA is very effective for individuals with autism.

Activity reinforcer—a favorite activity is rewarded for positive behavior.

APE—adaptive physical education is an individual program of developmental activities suited to the capacities of a student with a developmental disability.

Alternative communication system—another way for a nonverbal individual to communicate, such as signing, PECS, representative objects, motoric gesturing, or an electronic communicator.

Antecedent—what causes a behavior.

ASD—autism spectrum disorder.

Autism—a neurologic disorder appearing in the first three years of life that affects brain functioning and results in language, cognitive, and social deficits and a restricted repertoire of activities and interests.

Aversive—punishment or abuse such as squirting, shocking, and hitting to extinguish a behavior.

Avoidance behavior—behaviors used to keep from doing a disliked task; for example, an avoidance behavior of Derek's is signing "toilet" to leave a reading lesson.

Backward chaining—breaking down an activity into steps that are taught in sequence, beginning with the last step first.

Behavioral intervention plan—a document that is part of a student's IEP that identifies problem behaviors, has goals for decreasing behaviors and increasing desired behaviors, and includes interventions when specific behaviors occur.

Behavior management—a plan for changing behavior through consistent consequences.

Behavior modification—a model of behavioral change with reinforced learning or operant conditioning.

Behavioral supports—cues or prompts that help an individual achieve success.

CARS—Childhood Autism Rating Scale is an excellent diagnostic tool developed by Eric Schopler of the TEACCH program.

Chaining—breaking down an activity into steps and teaching the steps in sequence (task analysis).

CHAT—The Checklist for Autism in Toddlers is a screening tool that should be used by pediatricians at a child's eighteen-month well-baby appointment.

Compliance training—another term referring to discrete trial training.

Conjoint therapy—two therapies happening at the same time (such as occupational and physical).

Consequence—what follows a behavior. Ideally, negative consequences should follow negative behavior and positive consequences, such as praise, should follow positive behavior.

DDD (Department of Developmental Disability)—a state agency that is part of DSHS that assigns a case worker to qualified clients to help them access the services they need.

DSHS (Department of Social & Health Services)—state agency that provides Medicaid (medical coupon) and food stamps to those who meet the criteria.

Differential reinforcement—uses positive reinforcement for good behavior while ignoring unacceptable behavior.

DTT (Discrete Trial Training)—a behavioral teaching method that repeatedly presents a specific task to an individual and rewards successful responses.

DVR (Department of Vocational Rehabilitation)—this is a state agency that helps clients to become employed when they are no longer in their public school programs.

Echolalia—noncommunicative speech in which the person merely repeats what he or she hears, often in response to a question.

Extinction—ignoring a behavior to decrease it.

Fading—gradually lessoning or "fading" support that is required to help the student or client successfully complete a task. It may start by physically moving the hands, to grasping the wrist, to touching the elbow, to pointing, to verbal request, to written assignment, to complete independence.

Floortime—therapy developed by Stanley Greenspan in which the therapist or caregiver gets down on the floor with the child and copies his or her activities in an attempt to engage the child.

Functional behavioral assessment—this process determines why a problem behavior is occurring so that interventions can be implemented to prevent unwanted behavior such as aggression.

Generalization—the ability to take what is learned in one setting, such as school, and use it in another setting, such as home.

Gliadomorphins and casomorphins—peptides that are released from the partial digestion of gluten and dairy products, respectively. They are often referred to as food opioids, and some believe they cause symptoms of autism.

Hypersensitivities—a higher-than-normal reaction to sensory input. Tactile and auditory are common hypersensitivities.

IDEA (Individuals with Disabilities Education Act)—a law enacted in 1997 and updated in 2004 ensuring everyone the right to public education regardless of their disability.

IEP—Individual Education Plan is a document developed by a student's education team that could include the teacher, OT, PT, SLP, and psychologist. It includes current levels of performance, annual goals, short-term objectives, and a list of services that are required to meet the needs of the student.

IFSP—Individualized Family Service Plan, under part C of IDEA, is a program that awards grants to states to provide early intervention services to infants and toddlers who have disabilities or developmental delays.

Operant conditioning—the basis of behavior modification that uses consequential responses for changing behavior,

OT—occupational therapist- helps the client build skills that will optimally enable them to be employed and better cope in their environments by overcoming sensory integration dysfunction.

PECS—Picture exchange communication system is an alternative communication system in which the child first gives a picture of a desired object to receive it and then is taught to construct "picture" sentences to increase his or her ability to communicate.

PT (physical therapist)—those with autism may have gait or posture problems that can be improved with physical therapy.

Reinforcers—consequences that strengthen the behavior they follow; rewards. They should be faded as able so the behavior becomes independent.

Sensory integrative therapy (SIT)—occupational therapists use this therapy to treat sensory integrative dysfunction. The goal is to improve the tolerance of sensory input that is troubling to an individual with sensory integration deficits.

SLP (speech and language pathologist)—specialist who helps those with autism to better communicate with whatever means are most appropriate for the individual.

SLT—speech and language therapy is done to improve the ability to communicate; it is appropriate for those who are verbal or nonverbal.

Social stories—a way of communicating with a child to help him or her understand different concepts or situations and decrease anxiety. Social stories can even be a series of pictures or photographs for children who cannot yet read.

SSI (Social Security Income)—federal benefits that supplement living expenses for those who are disabled.

Stimming—self-stimulation such as rocking, flapping, finger flicking, or spinning.

Task analysis—breaking down a skill into steps that can be more easily taught.

Transition—changing from one task or place to another. This is often difficult for those with autism. Transition is also the job training done at high school between the ages of eighteen and twenty-one.

www.ingramcontent.com/pod-product-compliance
Lightning Source LLC
Chambersburg PA
CBHW031506270326
41930CB00006B/272